ShagMail.com presents...

The Best of
Bizarre News

www.bizarrenews.com

This book is dedicated to all those
readers who dare to dance to the beat
of a different drummer.

* * * Table of Contents * * *

Acknowledgments and thanks...

Putting this book into print has truly been a collaborative effort. First, much thanks needs to go to the management team at ShagMail.com for allowing me the freedom to pursue the stories and giving me full reign to express myself in just about any way a person could dream.

But the thanks need to precede management. While growing up, my father always drummed into me that I could do whatever I put my mind to doing. Although I sincerely doubt that he envisioned his son interviewing alien abductees, his words of encouragement are still with me long after he has since passed from this world. Growing up in an environment that encouraged the notion that anything was possible, and then actually finding a job that proved that anything truly was possible, led to this book.

Then there is my wife. How many women could possibly be secure enough to let their husbands visit brothels, travel the country in search of the bizarre and do so with bemused support? Also, there are the "stringers" who have so helped in pointing me to stories. Paula distinguishes herself as one of the most astute guiding beacons of bizarreness. My fellow editors have supported me personally and given me hours of critique as to what "bizarre" actually means. For TZ, (editor of LaffaDay), "bizarre" lands firmly between the knees and belt buckle. For Chadwick, (editor of Up Yours!) "bizarre" meant finding the more ignorant ways criminals attempted to ply their trade. Clean Laffs Joe thought that eating ice cream with a spoon qualified.

Mixed-up Cartoon Videos Not a Laughing Matter

DUBAI, United Arab Emirates - The Scooby Doo-doo hit the fan when a shop mistakenly sold porn videos as a promotion for children's chocolate candy. Parents were outraged when they discovered the films that were supposed to be cartoons turned out to be porn movies. Khamis Mohammed al-Suweidi explained in an open letter published in the Al-Ittihad newspaper that he had to dart to the video recorder and hit the off button when he saw eye-popping action and "obscene scenes that encouraged homosexuality". The Dubai police have seized about 400 cassettes and are still investigating the matter.

Alien Fetish?

WASHINGTON, DC - The Center For UFO Studies (CUFOS) has compiled a list of 13,528 U.S. women who believe that they have been abducted by aliens. Of this amount, 1,501 women reported that their panties had been kept by the aliens. It has not been revealed for what sinister purpose these aliens are hording underwear.

[That explains what happened to my wife's panties the other night when she came in at 3:00 a.m.!]

Queetzal The Alien Fathers Twenty

MURFREESBORO, Tennessee - Jeanne Robinson wants the world to know that she has been traumatized by aliens. According to her new book, A Quest to Understand Contact, she has undergone being raped by an alien at least twenty times. Each of these violent incursions resulted in a hybrid child. The alien rapist was the same gray "thing" named Queetzal. All of these abductions/rapes happened when she lived in Missouri's Ozark Mountains.

He's Too Sexy For His Liver Spots

TERRE HAUTE, Indiana - The Chippendale Dancers have a new threat and his name is "Disco Ernie." This 86-year-old male stripper is providing wrinkled yet provocative entertainment for more discerning parties. What started out as a joke 24 years ago is now thriving at 40 shows a year. Ernie can gyrate and shake his moneymaker while a stunned audience watches in disbelief. He has performed in nightclubs, drugstores, and once at a nursing home where he quotes, "But they didn't want me to take my clothes off; too many old people I guess."

60 Gallons and Still Pumping

ST PAUL, Minnesota - Harry Loomer, aka "Bloody Harry," earned the rare 60-gallon pin from the American Red Cross while on a visit to St. Paul, where he topped off his 60th gallon of donated blood. Since 1954, Loomer said he has donated blood 480 times in 21 states and about 80 cities, as well as in Canada and the Philippines. For reaching the 60-gallon mark last week, the St. Paul branch of the Red Cross had a little party for Loomer at which the staff sang an original tribute written to the tune of "I'm Just Wild About Harry." A large red and white cake had 480 lifesavers on it. Loomer, who claims he has not been sick in 50 years, says he is "going for 100 gallons.

Retiree Drives Across Country In Golf Cart

SOMEWHERE BETWEEN CONNECTICUT AND CALIFORNIA - What do you do if you're a retiree from California with nothing better to do with your time? If you're George Bombardier you like to take cross-country roadtrips in a golf cart. Bombardier lives in a trailer and can't do much with his emphysema and heart problems, so for the past few years he has been driving to Connecticut in a golf cart to see his kids. Among the amenities he carries with him are a television, radio, tape player and makeshift bed. This most recent trip will make his fourth circuit in two years.

[Bizarre News readers will not be surprised to learn that old George is also a divorcee.]

Somebody Cancel Her Research Grant

Irene Pepperberg is outstanding in the field of wasting money. A visiting professor of animal behavior at the Massachusetts Institute of Technology, Pepperberg is teaching a parrot how to surf the Internet. "Parrots are very social creatures," she says, but people who own them "leave them alone eight or nine hours a day." She says that leads to boredom and stress, and that leads to behavioral problems. She is developing special bird-enabled software, "InterPet Explorer", to make it easier for the animals to find sites of interest, such as those showing wildlife and music, or perhaps even chat rooms populated only by animals.

German Judge Makes Immaculate Ruling

A German woman's claim that her child was the result of an immaculate conception has been backed by a judge who said he could not rule out divine intervention. The judge concluded: "I can't rule out the possibility of divine intervention by God." Birgit Weiss, 45, told the court that she had not had sex with anyone else after the relationship with her former husband broke down - and yet genetic tests showed the child was not his. Her estranged husband accused her of trying to defraud him of child maintenance money.

Man Sets Record for Loudest Belch

LONDON, England - Paul Hunn was sure to have made his mum proud recently when he set a record for the world's loudest burp, which will be entered into the Guinness Book in October. The burp was measured at 118.1 decibels, which is reported to be a similar volume to a pneumatic drill or a jet engine at take-off. According to Hunn, "It's a winner down at the pub but it's not such a hit with women. My girlfriend's only just getting used to it." Hunn concluded by saying that "nobody in the world can touch me at burping, I've just got a natural talent for it."

Man Receives $310,000 for Disturbing the Peace

CHICAGO, Illinois - Jeffrey Marthon, 54, will receive $310,000 from his condominium association for trying to evict him because he has Tourette's Syndrome. Marthon's symptoms include involuntary foot stomping and yelling, which has kept his neighbors up numerous nights. Marthon filed a discrimination suit in federal court last year against the condominium association after the group sought to stop him from disturbing the neighbors or move from his condo, where he and his wife have lived since 1986. A federal judge dismissed Marthon's case after the two sides reached agreement.

Football Sized Tumor Removed From Man's Face

MIAMI, Florida - Doctors at the University of Miami/Jackson Memorial Hospital spent 10 1/2 hours removing the 18-inch tumor from a 37-year-old Haitian peasant farmer. Dieuvius Morancy told doctors he had been living with the football-sized tumor protruding from his face for two or three years. According to doctors, the benign tumor, called a meloblastoma, probably began growing 20 years ago

which he was
the dangerous sport of sky
When he was sent twisting through the
the ground at over 60 mph. Thomas was a member
of the Headcorn Parachute Club in England and was described by friends as "a very proficient jumper." The club's chief instructor, Peter Sizer, who was on the plane with Thomas, said, "We try to make the sport as safe as possible but unfortunately tragic accidents do happen."

[Surprisingly, sky-surfing has a much lower mortality rate than sky-hockey.]

Bigamist or Bigamister?

Follow closely, this gets a little complicated. Katherine is an Irish expatriate who used to be a man named Damien. She(?) is married to a man in Norfolk, VA named Pat who used to be a woman named Patricia. According to federal prosecutors, Katherine is in the country illegally and changed her gender to marry Pat who changed his gender to hide from his former spouse, John Martin, whom he had never divorced. Since Pat is still legally married to another man, his marriage to Katherine is not binding, and now both of them are under indictment for defrauding the Immigration and Naturalization Service. If they're really unlucky the Feds might throw in polygamy as well.

[Thanks to APBnews from whom the facts were unceremoniously stolen.]

ENGLAND - As if skydiving was not dangerous enough, try strapped to a surfboard! Nigel Thomas learned the hard way when the experienced skydiver plunged 15,000 feet to his death after his emergency parachute became tangled with a surfboard to which he was strapped. Thomas, 36 was demonstrating the art of air surfing to dozens of spectators before hittin the property," said an attorney for the Florida Club. "If you built a house next to a railroad track, would you expect the trains to stop coming?" questioned farm owner Paul Thompson. Thompson's lawyer said the charges are "hogwash" and that his client and his partner were there first.

Texas Men Accidentally Repossess Two Kids

HALTOM CITY, Texas - Three men attempting to repossess a minivan were arrested for towing it away with two children still buckled inside. The father jumped onto the side of the moving tow truck and flagged down a police officer. The father, his 2-year-old son and 5-year-old daughter were unharmed. "They were extremely traumatized by the ordeal," Detective Dennis Ochs said. The owner of the auto recovery business was charged with aggravated kidnapping and aggravated assault. The repo men were charged with aggravated kidnapping.

[Thanks to Diane W. who put me on the trail of this one.]

Posing For a Picture Poses Even Bigger Problem for Man

LaPORTE, Indiana - A snapshot quickly turned into a mug shot for a 38-year-old man after a film developer recognized pictures of the man's indoor garden as marijuana. The film processor at Martin's Supermarket in South Bend contacted authorities because the freshly developed pictures showed what appeared to be a marijuana growing operation. Brian Davis pleaded guilty in LaPorte Circuit Court to a Class D felony of maintaining a common nuisance. LaPorte Metro officers confiscated 39 nearly mature marijuana plants.

3

Between the Sheets

Let's face it; there will never be a shortage of humorous sex stories. There is something universally humbling about our obvious frailties when it comes to affairs of the heart. Our society has placed such importance on sex that it has permeated everything from bratwurst to college selection. In our pursuit for sexual gratification we have engaged in a tapestry of augmentation, mutilation, fetishisms, and, of course, my favorite: the pursuit of matrimonial bliss! When I realized that I was no longer the most depraved man on the planet I was relieved, but my journey to the darker side of the gender wars has given me a whole new respect for celibates.

Inflamed Penis Amputated

KUALA LUMPUR, Malaysia - It seems that every other issue a penis story pops up to grab the imagination of our editors. This time Bizarre News has uncovered the plight of 23-year-old Siva Kumar who had to undergo an emergency surgery after suffering an extreme allergic reaction to a new spermicidal cream used inside the condom. The reaction caused such severe swelling that doctors had to amputate a large portion of his inflamed penis.

Viagra Hard On The Neighborhood

BONN, Germany - Anna and Kurt Glitscher are being sued by local neighbors. The reason? It seems that their aged dog is up to some very old tricks. The Don Juan doggie is accused of getting six bitches pregnant in one madcap week of canine passion. The Glitschers are not innocent bystanders. They have been feeding their dog Viagra.

Wife Sues For Divorce After Sexual Rebuff

BALTIMORE, Maryland - A wacky newlywed attacked her husband in a rage after he refused to have sex one more time with her. Why? Apparently the couple had already had sex four times and her husband was, "tired from working all day." Police were called to the scene after objects were thrown through windows and loud arguments during her enraged aftermath. She is suing on the grounds of sexual incompatibility.

[Heck, only four times? When I was a kid I dreamed that I nailed Charlie's Angels three times each.]

Genitalia Needs Blowing Up

SYDNEY, Australia -An Australian research team studying insects had trouble identifying the sex of the little creatures so they decided to do something about this nasty problem. They invented a device dubbed, The Phalloblaster. This is no ordinary machine. It actually inflates the genitalia to a size that makes identification easier. The machine costs $3500.

[I do believe that Austin Powers had one of these.]

Update On Booty Babe

NEW YORK, New York - Just to update the story on the woman who sued her surgeon for putting breast implants into her butt, a jury awarded her $30,000 because the doctor departed from "good and accepted practices." The former go-go dancer was horrified as her butt looked like two breasts. The jury was comprised of four men and two women.

Fun In The School Yard?

SALISBURY, Maryland - A 10-year-old boy has been charged with assault for allegedly snapping girls' bras. The Pittsville Elementary pupil was accused of assaulting five girls, ages 8 to 11, earlier this month. He was suspended from school for three days. The boy was charged with four counts of assault for allegedly snapping girls' bras and one count of sex offense for allegedly touching a girl's buttocks.

[When asked why he did these things, he replied "I want to be President one day."]

Spontaneous Orgasms Cause Distress

LONDON, England - A medical journal, The Lancet, recently reported a rare condition of a case of "spontaneous multiple orgasms." It seems a 44-year-old woman would undergo multiple orgasms when doing routine household chores like laundry. The report continued to outline that extreme distress was caused to the woman due to the uncontrollable nature and intensity of the feeling. She was eventually treated with a medication normally used on epilepsy patients and she is now orgasm-free.

[And this is a good thing?]

Prostitutes Can Dress Down For Their Job

MADRID, Spain - If you're involved in the world's oldest profession, I think it's time to move to Madrid! Yep, they protect the rights of all prostitutes to wear little clothing, because it is their "work uniform." The police chief was trying to get a proposal passed that would charge prostitutes with the offense of indecent exposure. It was voted down because..."prostitutes should not be ordered to cover up because they are simply wearing the uniform of their profession."

Guaranteed To Reduce Travel Stress

AMSTERDAM - Your flight was delayed, you are tired, stiff and irritable, but if you are flying into or through Amsterdam's Schiphol Airport you can kiss that stress goodbye. A Dutch brothel chain is hoping to open a branch inside the airport next year. A visit to the Yab Yum Caviar Club will get you champagne, caviar and a relaxing massage. Plus, there are other services a stressed traveler can opt for. Prostitution is legal in the Netherlands, where the sex industry turns over an estimated $920 million annually.

Drop The Pounds...Add The Inches

NEW YORK, New York - New proof of the ultimate nightmare. Eating all that fatty food, saturating your blood with cholesterol and hardening your arteries can also shorten your penis. That's according to Dr. J. Francois Eid, Director of the Male Sexual Function Unit of New York Presbyterian Hospital. Blood supply is reduced when your arteries become lined with cholesterol. And your penis needs fast-moving blood flow to become erect. Says Dr. Eid, "[Overweight] men carry their weight at their abdomen, and this shortens the shaft...for every 35 pounds of weight loss, there is an apparent increase in penile length of 1 inch."

[If I could get down to about 65 lbs. I'd have to have all of my pants legs widened.]

Accident Victim Given Viagra to Rectify Wrong Dong

HONK KONG - A 52-year-old Hong Kong man, who said being hit by a motorcycle hurt his sex life, has been awarded a year's supply of Viagra as part of his court settlement. The South China Morning Post reports the judge awarded Cook Chan Kwuntak $550 to purchase the medication. The money is part of a $320,000 compensation package for Chan, who was hit by a motorcycle in June 1997. Chan originally asked for $5,500 worth of Viagra -- enough for a 10-year supply - to solve his sexual problems. But the judge ruled there was no reasonable evidence a 10-year treatment was necessary. This is the first time a Hong Kong court has awarded money for Viagra.

Citizens Against Breast-Feeding Protest

You're all incestuous perverts, according to Citizens Against Breast-Feeding. That's right, you read it in Bizarre News. According to chairwoman Tess Hennessy, "Monica Lewinsky's oral gratification received from President Clinton had a direct relationship to her demented childhood slurping mother's milk. Ask any psychologist." A small but determined knot of women waved placards outside LA's Staples Center Tuesday. One male supporter pointed out, "We wouldn't be having these arguments about the fundraiser at the Playboy Mansion if men like Hugh Hefner hadn't made millions from exploiting the incestuous dependency on the breast induced by encouraging people to suck their mothers' nipples."

Nude Cricket Players Warned For Showing Off Wickets

LONDON, England - A West Yorkshire police officer broke up a four-man game of nude Cricket at the Scholes Cricket club near Huddersfield after receiving complaints from residents. According to a spokesman for the West Yorkshire police, "Nobody was arrested, it was just a matter of giving them some advice regarding their conduct." Perhaps it was about what direction their foul balls were going.

Finally! A Vacuum Women Really Want

WASHINGTON, DC - Score one for the fight against female impotence. The FDA has just approved the Eros system, which was designed to increase blood flow to the clitoris. Simply put; it's a small tube attached to a suction cup that runs on batteries. Once the clitoris becomes properly engorged, the apparatus is removed, and.... A prescription is required, but there are no reported side effects.

[Three speeds: slow, medium, and who needs a man?!]

Oh, Baby!

STAFFORD, England - Coworkers wanted to do something special for Louie Holiman on his 50th birthday, so they threw him a party. They hired an exotic dancer to pop out of a cake. Louie got the shock of his life when his daughter popped out of the cake in the buff. She apparently did not know her father was the "jolly good fellow." The shock proved too much for the birthday boy and he dropped dead from a heart attack.

Just Call Him Bishop Naughty

NEW YORK, New York - Here's an award-winning career change; from bishop to cybersex writer. John Shelby Spong, former leader of the Diocese of New Jersey will be writing a new monthly column that will address issues of sexuality and how they relate to religion. "It's an attempt to discuss sexuality in a serious way... some people are treating this as some sort of salacious thing," remarked Spong. His new site ThePosition.com is being set up by former Penthouse editor, Jack Heidenry where the first issue questions if the Ten Commandments are biased against women.

[Hey, it's all in the name in higher spirituality, right?]

Woman Shocked At Husband's Work

ROME, Italy - How do you stop your wife from "enjoying herself" with her favorite sex toy? Electrician Antonio Murano had an idea. He booby-trapped his wife's gizmo to discharge a powerful electrical charge when she applied it to her private parts. She has since sued for divorce on the grounds of incompatibility.

[I wonder if he used to rub his feet on a carpet and then touch his wife?]

They'll Plump Your Pillows Too

BUCHAREST, Romania - In order to increase business due to the economic depression, a group of Romanian prostitutes is trying to lure clients by offering to do household chores. So not only will they perform sexual favors for the clients, but they will make the bed afterwards and serve them breakfast. "We had to invent something because people don't have money and clients are rare. After solving the sexual problem, the girls clean and cook for free. All on the house," said a "sexual agent" in Bucharest. It was not mentioned if the chores are performed in the nude or if the prostitutes do windows.

Nude Hitchhiker Pinched By Cops

GASTONIA, North Carolina - A 43-year-old female hitchhiker got a free ride to jail when she stripped to attract a ride. Hamza Schwenking-Ben, of Nuremberg, Germany, said she left Georgia about a week ago and was hitchhiking and walking her way along Interstate 85, hoping to meet a friend who lives in Virginia. Schwenking-Ben was picked up by a state trooper and charged with indecent exposure while she was standing at an exit ramp carrying her coat, a change of clothes and a passport. Officials said at least eight motorists called 911 on their cell phones instead of stopping.

100 Years Old And Still Frisky

BERLIN, Germany - What do you do if the spark goes out of your marriage? After being married 69 years, Heidi Berger decided to call it quits from her husband Hans. In papers filed in court, Heidi cited a lack of sex for grounds for divorcing. Heidi is 100 and Hans is 101.

Kings Island Reveals New Monica Ride

The Cincinnati Enquirer reported the revealing story of an impromptu sexual rendezvous in a Paramount's Kings Island photo booth. Elizabeth Whitaker, 24, and Aaron Caudill, 28, face charges of public indecency after the sex act was seen at 8 p.m. on a monitor outside the booth. Police reports indicate the couple noticed the photo booth as they entered the park that morning. Caudill "casually mentioned to his girlfriend that she could give him oral sex in this photo booth." Whitaker stated they had no idea the monitor was stationed outside of the booth. After snapping a photo of his favorite pose, Caudill realized what had happened, ran outside and tried to cover the image on the monitor with his hands.

Male Surprise In The Mail

HEILBRONN, Germany - Move over Lorraine Bobbit. There is a new snip in town. Hotheaded Helga Frosch was jailed recently for slicing her husband's penis off while he was sleeping (one could assume he woke up!). She fled their apartment to a hotel, gift wrapped the appendage and mailed it to husband Hans' mistress. When apprehended by German police, Helga reportedly said, "He'll never cheat on me again now that his feature attraction is stuffed in a jar of formaldehyde."

You Want Fries With That Shake?

SALEM TOWNSHIP, Pennsylvania - For the person that is always on the go, the Climax Gentleman's Club in Salem Township, near Pittsburgh, has been providing a drive-thru peep show service since April. Drivers can pull up to a window at the back of the club and show proof that they are 18 or older and pay $5 per minute. Then they pull up to a second window and watch a nude dancer for the amount of time they paid for. According to Barbie, a stripper at the club, most customers pay for two to three minutes, but one man paid $100 for 20 minutes. Township supervisor Ed Gieselman helped write a 1998 ordinance to regulate strip clubs. He called the drive-thru an advertising gimmick designed to generate publicity.

Stripper Claims T&A Not The Same

NEW YORK, New York - A former exotic dancer has filed a medical malpractice suit against Dr. Elliot Jacobs. It seems she went to this surgeon to add some shape to her rather flat behind...ten years ago. Well, Jacobs used silicon breast implants to augment her behind and she has suffered for years an uncomfortable feeling whenever she sits down. Jacobs' lawyer, Paul Paley has called the charges, "asinine."

Breast Implant Listed as Valuable Asset for Tax Exemption

COPENHAGEN, Denmark - Apparently, a tax appeals board in Denmark believed that breast implants were such a "valuable asset" to a massage parlor that they allowed the surgery to be tax deductible. The board reportedly decided that the surgery represented a "legitimate investment," which is backed up by the Danish corporate tax law that states that investments to improve or maintain facilities for running a business are tax-deductible.

4

Bizarre Laws, Customs & Holidays

Does anyone remember watching the Schoolhouse Rock episode about the making of a law? You know, the one featuring the cartoon of the sad little bill with his blue ribbon singing, "I'm just a bill. Yes I'm only a bill, and I'm sitting here on Capitol Hill?" After I read the following "worthy" laws carefully penned by our forefathers, it became perfectly feasible that all laws really did begin as singing cartoons! Why these came into existence is one question, but the better question is why are they still around? I think I'll go find "Bill" and ask him if he knows the answer to this riddle.

Bizarre Laws

ARIZONA

There is a possible 25 years in prison for cutting down a cactus.

Donkeys cannot sleep in bathtubs.

It is unlawful to refuse a person a glass of water.

Hunting camels is prohibited.

Any misdemeanor committed while wearing a red mask is considered a felony (This goes back to the days of the Wild West).

You may not have more than two dildos per household.

JANUARY IS...

January is... National Careers in Cosmetology Month

January is... National Eye Health Care Month

January is... National Fiber Focus Month

January is... National Hobby Month

January is... National Soup Month

January is... Hot Tea Month

January is... Oatmeal Month

January is... Prune Breakfast Month

January 27... Punch the Clock Day

January 31... Child Labor Day

OREGON

It is legal to smoke marijuana on your own property! You just can't sell it or buy it.

Patients do not have the right to know the details about any written or oral discussion of their medical treatment that is not recorded voluntarily in their chart by the nurse or doctor.

One may not bathe without wearing "suitable clothing," i.e., that which covers one's body from neck to knee.

It is illegal to use foul or suggestive language during sex.

You may not pump your own gas in service stations.

Canned corn is not to be used as bait for fishing.

FEBRUARY IS...

February is... National Blah Buster Month

February is... National Embroidery Month

February is... National Grapefruit Month

February is... Responsible Pet Owner Month

February is... Return Carts to the Supermarket Month

February is... Creative Romance Month

February is... International Twit Award Month

February 1 is... Serpent Day

February 4... is Create A Vacuum Day

February 6... is Lame Duck Day

February 9... is Toothache Day

February 17... is Champion Crab Races Day

February 20... is Hoodie Hoo Day

February 25... is Pistol Patent Day (Samuel Colt)

February 29... is National Surf and Turf Day

SOUTH CAROLINA

It is a capital offense to inadvertently kill someone while attempting suicide.

No work may be done on Sunday.

Two exceptions to the above law is the sale of light bulbs and tobacco.

It is perfectly legal to beat your wife on the courthouse steps on Sundays.

Merchandise may not be sold within a half mile of a church unless fruit is being sold.

By law, if a man promises to marry an unmarried woman, the marriage must take place.

All schools must prepare a suitable program for Francis Willard Day so that children may be taught the evils of intemperance.

The Fire Department in Charleston may blow up your house to create a fire brake.

OKLAHOMA

It is illegal to have the hind legs of a farm animal in your boots.

It's statutory rape for a man over 18 to have sex with a female under the age of 18, provided she's a virgin. If she's not a virgin, it is permissible, but the said person must be over 16. If both parties are under 18, the law does not apply.

Tattoos are illegal.

Whaling is illegal.

Women are forbidden from doing their own hair without being licensed by the state.

Women may not gamble in the nude, in lingerie, or while wearing a towel in Schulter, Oklahoma.

NEW JERSEY

It is against the law to "frown" at a police officer.

If you have been convicted of driving while intoxicated, you may never again apply for personalized license plates.

It is illegal to delay or detain a homing pigeon.

You may not slurp your soup.

To keep them from forming bad habits, it is illegal to feed whiskey or offer cigarettes to animals at the zoo in Manville, New Jersey.

MARCH IS...

March is... Foot Health Month

March is... National Furniture Refinishing Month

March is... National Frozen Food Month

March is... National Peanut Month

March 1 is... National Pig Day and Peanut Butter Lover's Day

March 5 is... Multiple Personalities Day

March 8 is... Be Nasty Day

March 9 is... Panic Day

March 11 is... Johnny Apple seed Day and Worship of Tools Day

March 15 is... Everything You Think Is Wrong Day

March 16 is... Everything You Do Is Right Day

March 18 is... Supreme Sacrifice Day

March 20 is... Festival Of Extraterrestrial Abductions Day

March 22 is... National Goof-off Day

March 24 is... National Chocolate Covered Raisins Day

March 27 is... National "Joe" Day

March 28 is... Something On A Stick Day

March 30 is... I Am In Control Day

March 31 is... Bunsen Burner Day and National Clams On The Half
Shell Day

ILLINOIS

You may be arrested for vagrancy if you do not have at least one-dol-
lar bill on your person.

It is a felony offense to eavesdrop on your own conversation.

You must contact the police before entering the city in an automobile.

The English language is not to be spoken.

Law forbids eating in a place that is on fire. - Chicago, IL.

It is an offense to feed whiskey to a dog. - Chicago, IL.

It is legal to protest naked in front of city hall as long as you are under seventeen years of age and have legal permits. - Chicago, IL.

It is illegal for anyone to give lit cigars to dogs, cats, and other domesticated animals kept as pets. - Zion, IL.

APRIL IS...

April is... National Anxiety Month

April is... National Humor Month

April is... National Welding Month

April 1 is... One Cent Day

April 2 is... National Peanut Butter and Jelly Day

April 3 is... Don't Go To Work Unless It's Fun Day

April 4 is... Tell-A-Lie Day

April 7 is... No Housework Day

April 9 is... Winston Churchill Day and Name Yourself Day

April 11 is... Eight-Track Tape Day

April 12 is... Look Up At The Sky Day

April 13 is... Blame Somebody Else Day

April 16 is... National Stress Awareness Day

April 17 is... National Cheeseball Day

April 19 is... Garlic Day

April 22 is... National Jelly Bean Day

April 23 is... Read Me Day and World Laboratory Animal Day

April 24 is... National Pigs In A Blanket Day

April 28 is... Great Poetry Reading and Kiss-Your-Mate Day

April 30 is... National Honesty Day

KENTUCKY

Any person who appears on a highway, or the street of any city that has no police protection, when clothed only in ordinary bathing garb, shall be fined not less than five dollars.

No person shall sell, exchange or possess living baby chicks, ducklings, or other fowl or rabbits which have been dyed or colored, nor sell or exchange baby chicks or other fowl under two months of age in any quantity less than six, except for any rabbit weighing three pounds or more may be sold at an age of six weeks.

[Well, now that we have that cleared up...]

Bees entering Kentucky must have a certificate of health.

Any person who displays, handles or uses any kind of reptile in connection with any religious service or gathering shall be fined not less than fifty dollars.

MAY IS...

May is... Better Sleep Month

May is... National Salad Month

May is... National Egg Month

May is... National Barbecue Month

May is... Date Your Mate Month

May is... Fungal Infection Awareness Month

May 1 is... Mother Goose Day and Save The Rhino Day

May 2 is... Fire Day

May 3 is... Lumpy Rug Day

May 7 is... National Roast Leg of Lamb Day

May 9 is... Lost Sock Memorial Day

May 11 is... Twilight Zone Day

May 13 is... Leprechaun Day

May 14 is... National Dance Like A Chicken Day

May 15 is... National Chocolate Chip Day

May 19 is... Frog Jumping Jubilee Day

May 23 is... Penny Day

May 24 is... National Escargot Day

May 26 is... Grey Day

May 29 is... End Of The Middle Ages Day

May 30 is... My Bucket's Got A Hole In It Day

May 31 is... National Macaroon Day

IDAHO

It is illegal for a man to give his sweetheart a box of candy weighing more than fifty pounds.

You may not fish on a camel's back.

It is an offense to ride on a merry-go-round on Sundays.

If a police officer approaches a vehicle and suspects that the occupants are engaging in sex, he must either honk, or flash his lights and wait three minutes before approaching the car. Coeur d' Alene, ID

CALIFORNIA

Animals are banned from mating publicly within 1,500 feet of a tavern, school, or place of worship.

No vehicle without a driver may exceed 60 miles per hour.

It is a misdemeanor to shoot at any kind of game from a moving vehicle, unless the target is a whale.

JUNE IS...

June is... Cancer In The Sun Month

June is... Adopt-A-Shelter-Cat Month

June is... Turkey Lover's Month

June is... National Accordion Awareness Month

June is... National Fresh Fruit and Vegetable Month

June is... Fight The Filthy Fly Month

June is... National Rose Month

June 1 is... Dare Day

June 2 is... National Rocky Road Day

June 3 is... Repeat Day

June 4 is... Old Maid's Day

June 5 is... Festival Of Popular Delusions Day

June 7 is... National Chocolate Ice Cream Day

June 8 is... Name Your Poison Day

June 10 is... National Yo-Yo Day

June 12 is... Machine Day

June 13 is... Kitchen Klutzes of America Day

June 15 is... Smile Power Day

June 16 is... National Hollerin' Contest Day

June 17 is... Watergate Day and Eat Your Vegetables Day

June 18 is... International Panic Day

June 19 is... World Sauntering Day

June 20 is... Ice Cream Soda Day

June 21 is... Cuckoo Warning Day

June 22 is... National Chocolate clair Day

June 26 is... National Chocolate Pudding Day

June 27 is... National Columnists Day

June 28 is... Paul Bunyan Day

June 30 is... Meteor Day

JULY IS...

July is... National Baked Beans Month

July is... National Ice Cream Month

July is... Anti-Boredom Month

July is... Hitchhiking Month

July 1 is... Creative Ice Cream Flavor Day

July 2 is... Visitation Of The Virgin Mary Day

July 3 is... Compliment Your Mirror Day

July 4 is... National Country Music Day and Tom Sawyer Fence Painting Day

July 5 is... Workaholics Day

July 6 is... National Fried Chicken Day

July 7 is... National Strawberry Sundae Day

July 11 is... National Cheer Up The Lonely Day

July 12 is... National Pecan Pie Day

July 13 is... Fool's Paradise Day

July 14 is... National Nude Day

July 15 is... Respect Canada Day

July 16 is... International Juggling Day

July 18 is... National Ice Cream Day and National Caviar Day

July 19 is... Flitch Day

July 20 is... Ugly Truck Contest Day

July 22 is... Rat Catcher's Day

July 25 is... Threading The Needle Day

July 26 is... All Or Nothing Day

July 27 is... Take Your Pants For A Walk Day

July 28 is... National Milk Chocolate Day

July 29 is... Cheese Sacrifice Purchase Day

July 31 is... Parent's Day

ALABAMA

It is illegal for a driver to be blindfolded while operating a vehicle.

It is illegal to wear a fake moustache that causes laughter in church.

Putting salt on a railroad track may be punishable by death.

Boogers may not be flicked into the wind.

ARKANSAS

By law, the Arkansas River can rise no higher than the Main Street bridge in Little Rock.

Arkansas must be pronounced "Arkansaw"

A law provides that schoolteachers who bob their hair will not get a raise.

A man can legally beat his wife, but not more than once a month.

Oral sex is considered to be sodomy.

Alligators may not be kept in bathtubs.

AUGUST IS...

August is... National Catfish Month

August is... Romance Awareness Month

August is... Foot Health Month

August 1 is... National Raspberry Cream Pie Day

August 3 is... National Watermelon Day

August 4 is... Twins Day Festival

August 6 is... Wiggle Your Toes Day

August 7 is... Sea Serpent Day

August 8 is... Sneak Zucchini Onto Your Neighbor's Porch Night

August 10 is... Lazy Day

August 12 is... Middle Child's Day

August 13 is... Blame Someone Else Day

August 15 is... National Relaxation Day & National Failures Day

August 18 is... Bad Poetry Day

August 25 is... Kiss-And-Make-Up Day

August 28 is... World Sauntering Day

August 30 is... National Toasted Marshmallow Day

August 31 is...National Trail Mix Day

UTAH

When a person reaches the age of 50, he/she can then marry their cousin.

It is illegal NOT to drink milk.

No one may have sex in the back of an ambulance if it is responding to an emergency call.

PENNSYLVANIA

It is illegal to have over 16 women live in a house together because that constitutes a brothel. However up to 120 men can live together, without breaking the law.

A special cleaning ordinance bans housewives from hiding dirt and dust under a rug in a dwelling.

You may not sing in the bathtub.

A person is not eligible to become Governor if he/she has participated in a duel.

Any motorist who sights a team of horses coming toward him must pull well off the road, cover his car with a blanket or canvas that blends with the countryside, and let the horses pass. If the horses appear skittish, the motorist must take his car apart, piece-by-piece, and hide it under the nearest bushes.

You may not catch a fish with your hands.

You may not catch a fish by any body part except the mouth.

OHIO

Women are prohibited from wearing patent leather shoes in public.

It is illegal to fish for whales on Sunday.

It is illegal to get a fish drunk.

The Ohio driver's education manual states that you must honk the horn whenever you pass another car.

Participating or conducting a duel is prohibited.

MASSACHUSETTS

A woman cannot be on top in sexual activities.

No gorilla is allowed in the back seat of any car.
[I can't even begin to guess what this is all about.]

Children may smoke, but they may not purchase cigarettes.

Tomatoes may not be used in the production of clam chowder.

Quakers and witches are banned.

Bullets may not be used as currency.

SEPTEMBER IS...

September is... Be Kind To Editors and Writers Month

September is... National Bed Check Month

September is... National Chicken Month

September is... National Mind Mapping Month

September is... National Papaya Month

September 1 is... Emma M. Nutt Day

September 2 is... National Beheading Day

September 5 is... Be Late For Something Day

September 11 is... No News Is Good News Day

September 12 is... National Chocolate Milkshake Day

September 13 is... Defy Superstition Day

September 15 is... Felt Hat Day

September 16 is... Stay Away From Seattle Day

September 18 is... National Play-Doh Day

September 22 is... Hobbit Day and Dear Diary Day

September 23 is... Checkers Day and Dogs In Politics Day

September 28 is... Ask A Stupid Question Day

September 29 is... Poisoned Blackberries Day

September 30 is... National Mud Pack Day

GEORGIA

It is illegal to use profanity in front of a dead body which lies in a funeral home or in a coroner's office.

You have the right to commit simple battery if provoked by "fightin'" words.

Members of the state assembly cannot be ticketed for speeding while the state assembly is in session.

Donkeys may not be kept in bathtubs.

Signs are required to be written in English.

No one may carry an ice cream cone in his or her back pocket if it is Sunday.

VIRGINIA

You can't have sex with the lights on and in any other position than the missionary position.

It is illegal to tickle women.

No one may wash a mule on the sidewalk. - Culpeper, VA

It is illegal to kick your wife out of bed. - Lebanon, VA

MINNESOTA

A person may not cross state lines with a duck atop their head.

It is illegal to sleep naked.

All men driving motorcycles must wear shirts.

It is the duty of any policeman or any other officer to kill any cat found running at large in any street, alley or public place in Hibbing, Minnesota.

OCTOBER IS...

October is... National Sarcastics Month

October is... National Apple Jack Month

October is... National Pickled Pepper Month

October 3 is... Virus Appreciation Day

October 6 is... Come and Take It Day

October 9 is... Moldy Cheese Day

October 12 is... Moment Of Frustration Scream Day

October 14 is... Be Bald and Free Day

October 16 is... Dictionary Day

October 17 is... Gaudy Day

October 21 is... Babbling Day

October 25 is... Punk For A Day Day

October 28 is... Plush Animal Lover's Day

October 29 is... Hermit Day

October 30 is... National Candy Corn Day

October 31 is... Halloween [A truly bizarre holiday.]

TEXAS

It is illegal to take more than 3 sips of beer at a time while standing.

You can be legally married by publicly introducing a person as your husband or wife 3 times.

A recently passed anti-crime law requires criminals to give their victims 24 hours notice, either orally or in writing, and to explain the nature of the crime to be committed.

The entire Encyclopedia Britannica is banned in Texas because it contains a formula for making beer at home.

NORTH CAROLINA

It's against the law to sing off key.

Elephants may not be used to plow cotton fields.
[Well, obviously.]

State law mandates that all couples staying in rooms for one night must be kept in a room with double beds, kept a minimum of two feet apart, and making love on the floor between the beds is strictly forbidden.

Women must have their bodies covered by at least 16 yards of cloth at all times. - Charlotte, NC

WASHINGTON

Mothers are not allowed to breast feed in public.

You cannot buy meat of any kind on Sunday.

Lollipops are banned.

It is illegal to pretend that one's parents are rich.

It is illegal to carry a concealed weapon that is over six feet in length. Seattle, WA

Dancing may not occur in the same establishment where alcohol is sold and consumed. -.Lynden, WA.

WISCONSIN

All yellow butter substitute was banned in the state, this included margarine. Since repealed.

Cheese making requires a cheese maker's license; Limburger cheese making requires a master cheese maker's license.

State Law made it illegal to serve apple pie in public restaurants without cheese.

The state definition of rape stated that it was a man having sex with a woman he knows not to be his wife.

No man can be in a state of arousal in public. - Kenosha, WI.

In the U.S., the Code of Federal Regulations declares it illegal for U.S. citizens to have any contact with extra-terrestrials or their vehicles.

NEW YORK

It is illegal to shoot at a rabbit from a moving trolley.

Flirting with a woman can earn a fine of $25. A second conviction is punishable by making the offender wear horse blinders in public.

It's illegal to speak to a person while riding in an elevator and you must fold your hands while looking forward.

You must purchase a license to hang clothes on a clothesline.

According to New York City statutes the following means of making a living are illegal: skinning horses or cows, burning offal (excrement), growing ragweed and burning bones.

CONNECTICUT

Neither Connecticut nor Rhode Island ever ratified the 18th Constitutional Amendment (Prohibition).
[Party on Connecticut!]

You can be stopped by the police in Connecticut for biking over 65 miles per hour.

It is against the law to dispose of used razor blades.

It is illegal for a man to kiss his wife on Sunday - Hartford, CT.

It is unlawful to walk backwards after sunset. - Devon, CT.

It is illegal for fire trucks to exceed 25-mph, even when going to a fire. - New Britain, CT.

Cattle branding in the United States did not originate in the West. It began in Connecticut in the mid-nineteenth century, when farmers were required by law to mark all their pigs.

WEST VIRGINIA

It is legal to beat your wife, but only in public on Sunday, on the courthouse steps. - Huntington, WV.

Firemen may not whistle or flirt with any woman passing a firehouse. - Huntington, WV.

No member of the clergy is allowed to tell jokes or humorous stories from the pulpit during a church service in Nicholas County, WV.

You may be punished by fine for wearing a hat inside a theater.

It is legal for a male to have sex with an animal as long as it does not exceed 40 pounds.

[I don't EVEN want to know how this one was mandated!]

MAINE

In Maine, it is illegal for a Police Officer to tell a person to have a nice day after pulling that person over in a car and issuing them a ticket.

After January 14th you can be charged a fine for still having your Christmas decorations displayed.

You may not step out of a plane in flight.

It is legal to bring shotguns to church in the event of an American Indian attack.

MONTANA

In Montana, it is illegal for married women to go fishing alone on Sundays, and illegal for unmarried women to fish alone at all.

It is a felony for a wife to open her husband's mail.

It is illegal to have sheep in the cab of your truck without a chaperone.

RHODE ISLAND

It is illegal to challenge someone to a duel, or to accept a challenge to a duel from someone, even if the duel is never fought. The penalty is imprisonment for one to seven years.

Any marriage where either of the parties is an idiot or lunatic is null and void.

Coasting downhill in a motorized vehicle with the transmission in neutral, or with the clutch disengaged is prohibited.

A penalty of $20 to $100 may be assessed for impersonating a town sealer, auctioneer, corder of wood, or a fence-viewer.

TENNESSEE

Tennessee recently passed a law making it legal to gather and eat dead animals off the road. - [Yummy.]

You can't hunt game from a moving automobile. The only notable exception to this law is whale hunting.

Any person crippling, killing or in any way destroying a proud bitch that is running at large shall not be held liable for the damages due to such killing or destruction.

The age of consent is 16, but 12 if the girl is a virgin.

More than 8 women may not live in the same house because that would constitute a brothel.

MICHIGAN

Michigan takes their rats seriously. You can collect a 10-cent bounty on every rat you bring into a town office.

It is legal for a robber to file a suit, if he or she is injured in your house.

Any person over the age of 12 may have a license for a handgun as long as he/she has not been convicted of a felony.

It is against the law to serenade your girlfriend in Kalamazoo.

Michigan law prohibits chaining an alligator to a fire hydrant.

COLORADO

You may not shoot a rabbit out of a second story window.

It is illegal to ride a horse while under the influence.

It is illegal drive a black car on Sundays in Denver.

Denver residents may not mistreat rats.

You cannot appear in public dressed in clothes "unbecoming" to one's sex - Durango, CO.

FLORIDA

In Florida, if you try to commit suicide and don't succeed you are free. However, if you do succeed, it is considered a felony.

State law prohibits men from being seen publicly in any kind of strapless gown. This also goes specifically for men in Miami.

Horse theft is punishable by hanging.

A special law prohibits unmarried women from parachuting on Sunday or she shall risk arrest, fine, and/or jailing.

You can be assessed a parking fee if you leave an elephant tied to a parking meter.

A man may not kiss his wife's breasts.

AUSTRALIA

In Victoria, it is illegal to wear hot pink pants after midday Sunday.

In Victoria, only licensed electricians may change a light bulb. The fine for not abiding by this law is 10 pounds.

It is illegal to roam the streets wearing black clothes, felt shoes and black shoe polish on your face as these items are tools of a cat burglar.

In Tasmania, until the Port Arthur Killings it was legal to own an AK-47 but not legal to be gay.

BIZARRE FESTIVALS

DOO DAH PARADE (U.S., Thanksgiving). A spoof version of the glittering Rose Parade held each year in Pasadena, CA, the Doo Dah Parade has deliberately become a byword in tackiness with badly-decorated floats, inept drill teams and a routine where businessmen in suits perform with their briefcases.

KING OF THE MOUNTAIN FESTIVAL (Norway, July). With a summit just 140ft above the surrounding plains, Mount Wycheproof in Victoria is registered as the lowest mountain in the world. This fact is celebrated annually with a foot-race up the mountain with each contestant carrying a sack of wheat weighing 140 lb.

LA TOMATINA (Spain). This festival dates back to 1944 when the fair at Bunol was ruined by hooligans hurling tomatoes at the procession. Now each year the town stages a 90-minute mass fight with 190,000 lbs of ripe tomatoes, an event which has relegated the annual fair to the status of a mere sideshow.

MOOSE DROPPING FESTIVAL (Alaska, July). Talkeetna plays host to an annual celebration of moose-droppings. Stalls sell jewelry and assorted knick knacks made from moose-droppings but pride goes to the moose-dropping-throwing competition where competitors toss gold-painted moose-droppings into a target, the winner being the one who lands his dropping closest to the center target.

SWINGING THE FIREBALLS (Scotland, New Year's Eve). Residents of Stonehaven march through the town swinging great balls of fire made from wire netting and filled with driftwood, pine cones, twigs and oil-soaked rags. The balls are thrown into the harbor to herald the New Year. The ceremony dates back to the Middle Ages when townsfolk tried to charm the sun from the heavens during the long, cold winter.

BIZARRE SUPERSTITIONS

Evil spirits can't harm you when you stand inside a circle.

Suspend a wedding band over the palm of the pregnant girl. If the ring swings in a circular motion it will be a girl. If the ring swings in a straight line the baby will be a boy.

A knife as a gift from a lover means that the love will soon end. [Especially if the knife is delivered to your back.]

If you use the same pencil to take a test that you used for studying for the test, the pencil will remember the answers.

The number of Xs in the palm of your right hand is the number of children you will have.

You must hold your breath while going past a cemetery or you will breathe in the spirit of someone who has recently died.

BIZARRE SEXUAL TRIVIA

If disconnected, the sex organs of an armadillo are still active.

Japan leads the world in condom use and are sold door to door by women.

The name of Wyoming's Grand Tetons mountain range literally means "Big Tits".

Every year, 11,000 Americans injure themselves while trying out bizarre sexual positions.

White women and those women with a college degree, in particular, are the most receptive to anal sex.

5

Genius... Not!

Some of my favorite Bizarre stories revolve around human error. We all secretly indulge our dark sides when we witness the simplest of tasks ending in abject humiliation. My theory behind why this is so appealing has to do with our own sense of relief. Relief because there is living proof that there is always someone else out there who can screw up in bigger and better ways. We can read about these people and adjust the yardstick for stupid. While I've never considered myself a Rhodes scholar; these people make me look like Einstein.

Not a Good Place to Take a Snooze

OMAHA, Nebraska - Sleeping in a garbage dumpster proved not to be a good idea for a Nebraska man Monday. Keith Quick, 28, was hospitalized after the dumpster he was sleeping in was emptied into a garbage truck and compacted several times. According to Omaha Fire Department spokesman Craig Schneider, it was not until several stops and several loads of trash later that the truck driver heard Quick calling for help. By that time he had been compacted "two or three times." Schneider went on to say that it took firefighters about an hour to dig the man out from the tightly compressed refuse packed into the hopper of the garbage truck. Miraculously he was not seriously injured.

[Yeah, but you can write that suit off.]

Woman In Jam Over Pregnancy

MOBILE, Alabama - Gretchen Radslaw is mad as all get out because she is pregnant and is suing a local chemist for $500,000. It seems Gretchen went to this chemist because he was selling a contraceptive jelly that was 98% effective in preventing pregnancies. Gretchen began diligently spreading the jelly on her toast every morning and after 3 months was pregnant. The suit stated that the chemist never told her that the "jelly" was not edible and that it needed to be applied to her vagina prior to intercourse.

[Why do these things happen in Alabama more than other places?]

The Ups And Downs Of Being A Janitor

BRISTOL, England - This little gem was in a local Chicago newspaper. It is not so newsworthy as it reveals a certain quirk unique to fellow English speakers across the pond. A janitor at a Marriott Hotel was fired for taking four days to clean an elevator. When asked why it took so long, before his dismissal he said, "There are twelve of them, one on each floor, and sometimes some of them are not there." He apparently thought that each floor had a different elevator and cleaned the same elevator 12 times.

This Story Sucks

HOUSTON, Texas - An unidentified woman was recently admitted to a Houston hospital after she had a run in with her high-powered vacuum cleaner. Her appliance was clogged and she looked into the attachment. The hose became unblocked and the sudden suction severed the optic nerve leaving her blind in one eye.

[OUCH!]

Surgeon's Career Ended By Store

DUBLIN, Ireland - A surgeon filed suit against a local store claiming that he had been impaired after walking into a trailer and hurting his back. He could no longer do heart surgery after the accident. His case was dismissed after the store's lawyer appealed to the judge's good sense. He pointed out that any surgeon who was careless enough to walk into a trailer that was 28 feet long, 8 feet high, equipped with a smoking barbecue and all the while blasting out music, should not be allowed near an operating table in the first place.

Goofy Disney Exec Remains Jailed For Porn

LOS ANGELES, California - Most people know about the former Disney Internet executive, Patrick Naughton who was caught soliciting sex from a 13-year-old girl while online and at work. Well he was sentenced to jail after being convicted and has been denied bail [and presumably access to a computer] while he goes through the appeal process. His defense indicated that he was under a great deal of stress and disturbed.

[Part of his punishment is to draw pants on old Donald Duck collectible cells.]

He Has Seen The Light

NEW ORLEANS - Reggie Dickerson and family are fine... just his ego is bruised after he burned down his home. How did he do it? In trying to determine if there was any gasoline in his gas can, Reggie used a lighter to look into it. And yes there was just enough to burn the house down.

[This guy gets the idiot of the week award.]

Lead In Pencil From Iron In Diet?

BRUSSELS, Belgium - Trucker Luc Duchateau thought he was just doing what the doctor ordered when he visited his local hardware store and purchased a bag of small nails. After his normal dinner, he began to swallow several of the nails whole. The 34-year-old patient was told that he needed more iron in his diet to improve his sex drive and figured this was the quickest way to improve performance. The metal cut into his stomach as he was rushed to the hospital.

[I am sure he would rather have nailed the nurse...]

Russian Wife Pierced By Enthusiastic Husband

MOSCOW, Russia - Gregori Vanechesky thought he had invented a great new bulletproof vest but he has to go back to the drawing board. This amateur inventor tested the vest on his wife and now the wacky Russian is a widower. That's right, she was pronounced dead on arrival at the hospital, as the vest did not prove to be bulletproof.

[One can only ask what "proof" he was drinking when he concocted his test plan.]

Crime Does Pay But Being Stupid Doesn't

WINNIPEG, Canada - Didn't your mother ever tell you not to jingle your pocket change while strolling through the ghetto? That's exactly the type of response a Canadian mugging victim received from Judge Charles Rubin. The 46-year-old Winnipeg resident was chastised by Judge Rubin for being a "stupid civilian, who admits that he was stupid," after two men approached him late one night. One of the men snatched the victim's money right out of his hand. Judge Rubin compared walking around in a bad neighborhood with money in your hand to "walking in the wolf enclosure at the city zoo with a pound of ground beef in your hand." The victim responded to the Judge's comments, saying that he was "insulted." The prosecutor is considering an appeal.

What A Way To Die

DRAYTON, Ontario - Three farm workers got in over their heads when they climbed into an 18,000-liter liquid manure tank and were overcome by the fumes. Henry Redekop, 23, Gary Ferrier, 32, and Eric Schulz, 33, were pronounced dead at the scene. The bodies were removed from the tank by firefighters wearing air tanks. The precise cause of the deaths has yet to be determined, however, police believe the men were killed by inhaling deadly methane gas when they climbed into the partially full tank to repair a faulty part.

[While tragic, this episode does lend credence to the proverb "to get one's self into deep sh!t."]

Man Rescued From Portable Toilet

HUNTINGDON VALLEY, Pennsylvania - Here's one that you just want to yell at the guy, "What were you thinking!" Authorities were dispatched to rescue a man who got stuck in a portable toilet. How? The genius lost his keys down the opening and decided he'd better go down and get them. Luckily for him, some kids were playing nearby and heard his cries for help. The police arrived to find the man stuck in the toilet's lower chamber up to his hips. The man, who was not identified, had taken off his shoes and pants for the unpleasant task. He told police he had been in the predicament for at least 45 minutes. The man was treated for cuts and bruises. Doctors also had to remove the toilet seat, which had become wedged around his torso.

Sleepy Thief

TRINIDAD - A would be thief in Trinidad broke into a house but was busted because he took a nap in the kitchen. Leroy Antoine, 54, was sentenced to five years in jail. Caught by the owner of the house, Nigel Balbickram, Antoine is a repeat offender with no less than 8 previous convictions.

[Antoine... find a new profession, you're creating too much paper-work for the cops!]

A Dog, A Drunk and A Missing Pinkie

BROOKLYN, New York - A pet owner was shocked to find his dog carrying, in his mouth, a severed human finger with a ring on it. A few hours later, Jose Cardenas solved the mystery by checking into a local hospital with his left pinkie missing. Cardenas, 42, told police he'd been drinking and had no idea how he ended up with only 9 digits. The finger couldn't be reattached.

[At least he got his ring back!]

Caught Left-Handed

TAIPEI - You have to give this Taiwan insurance salesman a hand for originality when he talked two friends into chopping off his left hand in an attempt to collect on $645,000 worth of insurance policies. Huang Chun-ming, 35, got liquored up before his friends chopped off his hand with a samurai sword. While at the hospital, Chun-ming tried to pass the injury off as a gruesome attack by a teenage motorcycle gang. One of Chun-ming's friends admitted to committing the act due to the fact that Huang had ran up gambling debts of T$20 million. Police report-edly found Chun-ming's missing hand inside his home.

Caller Screwed By Phone Sex Company

TROY, New York - What do you do when you are drunk and want to hear someone talk dirty to you? Ask Harold Reinke. It seems that after a hard night of partying, he called a European 900 sex line that charged $9.95 per minute. There was only one problem. The inebriated Reinke fell asleep while getting an ear full and woke up hours later still connected. The bill? Only $7,164.

Nothing to Wine About

LODI, California - Many people use alcohol to drown their sorrows. However, one California winery worker got more than he bargained for when he fell into a 23,000 gallon vat of red wine. Mario Flores, 31, apparently slipped through a hatch at the top of the container while taking liquid level measurements. According to Coroner Al Ortiz, the official cause of death is being withheld pending a microscopic exam of tissues and toxicology report. He concluded by saying "Drowning would look like the most likely cause."

[They're ruling out suicide as well considering Flores got out twice to urinate. Sorry, that was a little callous.]

Doctor Sued For Carving Initials On Woman's Abdomen

NEW YORK - Ladies, make note of the name Dr. Allan Zarkin and stay far away from him. Why? It seems that the good doctor is being investigated - and sued - for allegedly carved his initials on a woman's abdomen after performing a Caesarean section because he felt he had done such "a beautiful job." According to witnesses at New York's Beth Israel Medical Center, Dr. Zarkin etched the three-inch letters into the skin of new mother Linda Gedz as she lay sedated. Zarkin, dubbed "Dr. Zorro" by hospital staff, had no comment.

[And who said people no longer have pride in their work?]

Woman Stiffed After Sex

AKRON, Ohio - According to 44-year-old Karen Kershaw of Akron, the price of a used truck is $600 cash plus two sexual favors and four cartons of cigarettes (yes, cigarettes). These were the amounts to be paid to Rick Remmy, 39, only in the end she didn't get the truck. Now they're in Small Claims Court, where Karen wants her money back. A handwritten agreement outlined the values to be assigned to each item or act and bore what appeared to be Remmy's name at the bottom. Kershaw is asking for her money back and $14,700 in punitive damages. A Municipal Judge is expected to rule in the next week whether the "contract" is legitimate and whether Kershaw should be tried for prostitution.

Considerate Bank Robber Leaves Business Card

PLANTATION, Florida - Alfred Fiser will check his pockets a little more carefully after he dropped a business card and a blank check during a bank robbery near Fort Lauderdale. Fiser pulled an envelope from his shirt pocket after a teller at the World Savings Bank that he was robbing told him there were no envelopes to put the money in. Police used the items to trace Fiser to his home where they arrested him for grand theft and bank robbery.

Mechanic Gets Wrapped Up In Work

ALAMO, Michigan - Mechanic James Burns had a unique idea. Police said that he couldn't located a mysterious knock in a truck left for him to fix. So to get a better look, he asked a friend to drive the truck while he hung underneath so he could ascertain the exact source of the bothersome noise. Before he could tell anybody what the noise was, he managed to kill himself. He was found under the truck with his clothes and part of his body wrapped around the drive shaft.

Bad News for Alabama Belles

A federal appeals court has upheld an Alabama law banning the sale of artificial penises. The law was challenged last year by six women who either sell sex aids or said they need them to get the job done. A U.S. District Judge agreed saying it was "overly broad" and in violation of due process rights. But last week a three-judge, 11th Circuit panel overturned the ruling. They said the law, "is rationally related to the state's legitimate government interest in public morality." The penalty for selling or distributing a rubber dicks in Alabama? Up to one year in jail and a $10,000 fine.

[Cucumber farmers celebrate the ruling....]

Chestnuts Roasting on an Open Fire

Birthday boy Daniel Price was literally in the hot seat after a kiss-o-gram smothered his groin in baby oil and then set it on fire. The 17-year-old's party turned into a flaming nightmare when kiss-o-gram performer Rachel Prendergast, alias WPc Piddly, pulled down his trousers, then doused his privates in oil. Cheered on by guests she then whipped out a lighter and set fire to the oil as her party piece. According to Prendergast, the oil is only supposed to "give the punter a bit of a shock" with a warming sensation. But in this case, the flames ignited Daniel's boxer shorts and he started to burn out of control. A quick-thinking pal threw beer between his legs and he was rushed from his home in Stroud, Gloucestershire to a burn unit in Bristol.

6

The Best of Reader Comments

I know I've said this before but it bears repeating that without the dedicated readers of Bizarre News, I would have no column. It's the devotees to the strange and twisted that give my life direction. With all of the odd adventures and discoveries I've had, my readers out-shine everything. Some of these comments are so far out of left field that they merit special attention. I used to wonder if they allow patients to use laptop computers. I no longer question that. You'll notice that the reader comments are replete with spelling errors. I've left your comments exactly the way you wrote them so I could share the humor. I assume your mistakes were part of the joke right...?

Hey Lewis, I want to be a mortician when I grow up. What's wrong with that? Dead people don't complain.

[Too many Mickey Spillane novels for you.]

I just saw this headline in the Houston Chronicle online: "Death row prisoners launch hunger strike" Is it just me or is this not a problem?

[It is not only "not a problem," but a solution!]

you folks are just sick, nothing in all my life comes close to the per-version you propagate upon the innocents of the world.

[That's our job! Bringing the weird to your mail box.]

Damn you and your irresistibility!

[If only I used my power for good instead of evil, right?]

the bad man cut my gums. it hurts. i cant brush my teeth.

[Stop dating guys with braces.]

Lewis I am an 80 year old grandma. I love reading your Bizarre News. It brightens my day and makes me laugh. May your hands never wrinkle and your eyes never blur.

[Thank you. I've always had a way with the ladies.]

I'm so glad to see you understand that the juxtaposition of disfamiliar entities requires accurate balance of articulated definition.

[Mmmm hmmm.]

In Canada we have sex with aliens all the time. They're called "Americans"

[And don't think we don't appreciate it.]

I read Bizarre News today and it made my butt itch.

[Try an herbal cigarette.]

I just read your report of the Yale University study on the psychological effects of a "bad hair day." What happens if you are having a bad pubic hair day?

[Aren't they all?]

Hey Lewis, Are you my Daddy?

[I don't know. Do you have six toes on your left foot?]

Most snails can't ride motorbikes

An elephant's penis on average weighs sixty pounds.

[A helpful tip for anyone going on safari in the future.]

Gee whiz, another report on how all southerners are racist, tobacco-chewing Bubbas. Gosh, we've never heard that stereo-type before. By your reckoning, I should call all northerners loud, obnoxious assholes...

[So, you've been up North?]

I was taking a stroll in Louisiana, minding my own business, and got hit by panties thrown from a float, can I sue?

[It depends on if a girl was in them when you were hit.]

Have you noticed how talk shows are asking for more and more detailed problems? No more "Are you cheating and want to confess" it's "Are you cheating on your lesbian lover with her best friend or relative and both of you are grossly obese prostitutes?"

[Simple is out and complicated plots are in.]

I think your wife married you for the same reason my hubby tells everyone he married me - a life full of Cheap Entertainment!

[Who are you calling cheap?]

Lewis, as the remaining Alabama subscriber, I feel compelled to send you a note of encouragement...if there's one thing that we Alabamians know, (besides racism, inbreeding, illiteracy, and football) it's good journalism.

[Don't worry, I'll try to come up with a way to offend you.]

Why does your "writing" seem so hauntingly familiar?

[Because I used to be Walt Whitman in a previous life.]

I guess that sleep apnea thing is making you a little bitchy. You managed to insult overweight women, people with bad eyesight and the mentally challenged all in one letter. What, weren't there any people in wheelchairs within sight?

[It's true, I got a little carried away. I've been spending a lot of time with Chadwick. But hopefully today's letter will reconfirm my strong feminist sympathies.]

Women have been fighting in hand to hand combat for as long as war has been around. Ever hear of the Amazons, sh*t-head? They were a real group of people you know, not just something to wack off to while you watch Xena. There was even a female spy during WWII that parachuted into Germany, and then biked around, killing MALE Germans along the way as needed. As a black belt in Tae Kwon Do, I resent your *@$!%* attitude. Rest assured I could kick your fat ass any day of the week and twice on Sunday. As it is, I plan on unsubscribing from Bizarre News. I like the funny news, but I can live without your @*!$*@ attitude.

[I knew I was going to get some negative feedback on that article, but this is ridiculous.]

I request that you offend more groups and individual people in the next issue. For example, there's Pope John Paul... what's with that hair? And the Yankees. No, not the baseball team, those guys who live up North, And Eskimos and strippers named Chloe, and my sister in law.

[You misunderstand me. I try to be provocative, not overtly insulting. You want to talk to Chadwick, editor of Up Yours!]

I need an answer to a question I've been asking about for years. Why do straight men think it's so disgusting to see gay males kissing...but they would break their necks to watch 2 women kissing?

[If you don't know, I can't explain it.]

Hey I used to drive a cab in Colorado. I was scared all the time except for when that stripper ummm well never mind. Well, my brother is only about four feet tall, do you think, if I tried hard enough, that I could stuff him in the washer machine?

[Bizarre News is not responsible for copycat acts carried out by its readers. I just want to get that right out in the open.]

Why is it when a man talks dirty to a woman it is sexual harassment but when a woman talks dirty to a man it is $3.95 a minute?

[Because we're stupid.]

If Fred Flintstone knows the Brontosaurus ribs will tip his car over, why does he order them night after night?

[If you've ever had Brontosaurus ribs you wouldn't have to ask.]

Hey Lewis, They have "marriage tours" for American women too! They take a bunch of desperate American femmes to Ireland or elsewhere so they can find a willing male. Oh, and would any wealthy American woman care to marry an impoverished Canadian philosophy student?

[Whoever said romance is dead?]

I habe dem Zahnarzt gegessen. (German for "I ate the Dentist")

[Ich bin ein Berliner. (German for "I am a jelly donut.")]

I see an alarming situation here - If people kill all the 15 year olds who are possesed by demons, where will McDonalds get it's employees? Good thing that the Le Salon Sex Symbol in Canada was shut down. A hair stylist wielding a pair of scissors while doing an erotic dance has the potential of someone getting an eye poked out.

[An important safety tip. I'll pass that on to my wife.]

WHAT DO YOU MEAN YOU DON'T RULE HALF THE WORLD? THATS IT I WANT MY UNDERWEAR BACK!

[Then next time use a SASE.]

Hey Lewis, I was hoping to become a Gynecologist then my Dad said with all that schooling you'll always be in the Hole

Your latest issue may have set a record with references to 3 oxymora: Filipina virgins, Arkansas reader, and intelligent blondes.

My cat used to get high with us at parties. He would follow the bong around the room.

[Who said I don't have any subscribers left from Alabama?]

I just wanted to share this strange fact I still have trouble excepting. Tropical fish can survive for four months in human blood!

[What type?]

I think you are my father?
[I might be!]

a wop bop a loo bop a wop bam boom

I haven't been that disappointed in something since the time I saw my father naked.

I thought you mind find some of these rules interesting: At my friend's boarding school in California, girls are not allowed to bring bananas into their dorm rooms.

[Which school is this?]

Here in Pennsylvania plowing isn't considered a sport...until the 10th beer.

[Isn't anything a sport after 10 beers?]

I can tell you aren't from Louisiana, home of the wonderful cajun people. Their dogs names are pronounced the same, but the names are spelled Phideaux.

I went to a Lynard Sknyard/ZZ Top concert and the opening band was called the Screaming Cheetah Wheelies. Does that make any sense to you?

[No. I'm completely confused as to why you would go to a Lynard Sknyard/ZZ Top concert.]

Did you know that there is a fuel stop in Texas named, Texas Interstate Truck Stop & Auto Service Station, which proudly displays it's initials on a 60 foot high billboard along side interstate 20.

[I'm sorry. I just don't believe that. Please send a pic.]

"Did you spill any beer as you swung at him!?" That's what some wise-ass reporter shouted to Tonya Harding after her arraignment a few weeks ago. Tonya was arrested for beating up her current boyfriend and smacking him with a hubcap.

[That gentle flower is just misunderstood.]

Hey Lewis, Why do men have nipples?

[So women have something to nibble on.]

I slept with a Sumo wrestler in my past life...can you guess how I died?
[Hypertension?]

We learned in church that Lot's wife looked back and she turned into a pillar of salt. My Mom looked back once while she was DRIVING, and she turned into a telephone pole!

[That's God's wrath for you. Are you sure it was salt? It's been a while since I read that story, but wasn t she turned into a pillar of garlic?]

More fun than a stomach pump!

I have been trying to unsubscribe for over a week. i have been told by my employer we can not received any emails that do not pertain to my job. If i keep receiving this mail at work, i will lose my job.

[This is censorship...I think it is time to get a new job!]

Hey Lewis, the story about the sauna championships must be a little off... I've been in a 210 degree sauna before and lasted a good 10-15 minutes, and after sitting in the hot steam for a while, you get beaten with birch branches soaked in hot water.

[Was the person beating you wearing a leather bustier and garters? If so, I've been to that place before.]

About the new [Bubbles n Boobs] car wash in CA... you're telling me that they are charging $50 to give your CAR a hand job? Good Grief! What's the going rate for PEOPLE?

Hey Lewis, you know if there is such a thing as Karma, you are so screwed.

Your readers seem to be more bizarre than your news

[We noticed this as well]

I smell like cheese...

Hey Lewis, if you would like I will let you advertise on my melons!

[That depends...are you a farmer or a stripper?]

You rode the little short bus to school, didn't you?

[You got it, and the horse you rode in on as well]

I had a professor who did her dissertation on strippers. She even brought in pasties to show us how they're pasted on. She was a great professor.

[What class was this in?]

Lewis, I dont know about you, but i have breast implants in my butt and I'm loving them!

One of Kentucky's state parks is called BIG BONE LICK State Park. If you need groceries, you can go down the road a few miles to BEAVER LICK.

[The office is organizing a special expedition to this place.]

You're coming to Australia? What did we ever do to you?

Lewis, Do you think you could put your personal notes at the end of each newsletter instead of the beginning? It would make them easier to avoid. Thanks.

[Tough crowd.]

I have been reading Bizarre News for some time, and haven't gotten pissed about any of your observations yet. So, for my upcoming birthday, could you possibly write something crass about Jimmy Buffett or Star Trek?

[Star Trek was actually a propaganda campaign designed by the Communists in the 1960's. For that matter, so was Jimmy Buffett.]

loois, since starting to reed yor bizzar nuws, my iq has rised 50 poynts, plus i am mulch smartor

Hey, Lewis... My ass is twitching. You people make my ass twitch!

Regarding the house cleaning prostitutes in Bucharest-we do the same thing here, we just legalize it by calling it marriage!

You think going to a nudist camp is bad? Try being invited to a nude wedding. A friend of mine recently had the pleasure of being invited to such an event. The bride wore a veil, and the groom wore a hat.

[So, who was the best man, really?]

it has recently been determined that research causes cancer in lab rats.

It's your commentary that caused me to unsubscribe. It's not so much that you're crass: you're functionally illiterate.

[I don't think that's fair. My illiteracy is fully functional.]

I am BuenoCabra. I am a goat. Soon, I shall rule the world.

[A perfect example of what too much Bizarre News can do to a person.]

Tell me, how does a person get a live grenade embedded in their thigh, anyway?

[Maybe he was shot with one of those explosive shells during a training exercise. It could happen.]

You're doing fine. Just keep on doing what your therapist tells you and take your Prozac like a good boy. Mother

reading your newsletter made one thing clear. i must find a more suitable host body.

why does my dog hump the computer screen everytime i read your newsletters?

[Maybe he's trying to teach you something]

Alcohol and Calculus don't mix, so don't drink and derive.

[Cute.]

My mother grew up in the Amish community. She was not amish, but will tell you that Amish teenagers were the wildest bunch of kids in the community. It is exceptable (elders look the other way) behavior until they marry.

[Those Amish teens. You haven't seen anything until you've seen buggy drag racing.]

How many of our readers are hooked on crack, do you think? Lewis, you reflect the true nature of the world. I am applying for an exit visa now.

Ahhh, once again we meet, the ambrosial stuffs of fantasy, the great... Bizarre News!... an enema for your soul!

You are my dream stud! Marry me and I will bear your six-fingered, cross-eyed, webbed-feet children! We can all live together in a pretty little house in Alabama.

[Hey Sis, how many times do I have to say this, I am already married... to our cousin, remember?]

Do you know how a near sighted gynecologist is like a dog? They both have wet noses!

[There's one thing about Bizarre News readers. They have real class.]

Lewis, did your parents meet at their family reunion?

Lewis, my travels with the US Navy took me to the land down under a couple of times and there is a word that has been imbedded in my head since I first heard it: "Poofta" It's a slang word for a man that dresses like a woman. No fooling!

[I believe you. There are several American slangs which are not all that dissimilar.]

I don't know which is killing me faster. Your newsletter, or my daily intake of arsenic. Thanks to you, I now know this is a bad supplement.

I'll be right back - I've gotta go shave my butt...

I realy enjoy the email you send me and was very surprised to see the reference to "That's My Mama" which is a show I developed for Columbia in the 1970s. I didn't realize that anyone recalled it except Clifton Davis, Ted Lange and me.

Where did I put my mighty morphin power ranger lunch box? Lewis, can you help me?

First, it's a shame that oral sex carries a $2500 fine, but well done is definitely worth such a surtax.

I love it. Best screwball mailing list I have ever known.

My screen starts to shake and my toes curl up under my feet when ever I start to read your news letter. Explain please.

Do I have cancer?

Here in Kentucky you don't have to be any certain age to marry your cousin.

That does it! I'm getting my testicles pierced!
[Just go skinny dipping with snapping turtles]

Do I look fat?

Your list is like a bad accident...it hurts to look but ya just cant stop staring.

My brother has 3 testicles- i'll talk him into giving one to that man in Utica, NY- for a price, of course.

Lewis, your newsletter is the finest piece of literature ever penned.

unbefrigginlievable!

I think my dog is reading Bizarre over my shoulder.

If that Sassy Redheaded lass is single...I have all my teeth, but 3 are fake...can I get a date with her?

I love ya Lewis but if you're getting paid for this, it's too much! [Shhhhhhh!!!]

I make sure I tell all my friends about your site. Problem is after that, they no longer wish to associate with me.

where the hell do you come up with this stuff?

When I read Bizarre I get the feeling that I'm being tickled by 4 midgets with feathers.

My cat is dying with laughter. then again..it could be a hairball.

did u know pigs have orgasms that last up to 30 min...all I can say is "lucky pig"

[Bizarre readers are always enlightenting us---thanks.]

Top of the morning to you and all that crap, but bizarre is spreading like a nasty s.t.d over to the good old emerald isle.

I WILL $UE YOU, THIS MAGAZINE GAVE ME A WART ON MY ASS

[Careful! It can also make you sterile. I recommend wearing a lead apron while reading.]

AHH!!! why do spiders have 8 legs? it freaks me out

i can do stupid things.

[Please do them in the privacy of your own home.]

My fish can yodel!

[You should talk to the guy with the spider fetish.]

Goats all over the world are clutching their udders in shock and dismay. Wanton streams of goat milk flying everywhere is not a pretty site.

Daffy Duck, the well known cartoon animal, Is in fact, a LOON! Just look at the guy, he looks nothing like a duck, for one thing he is black, like a loon, and has a white ring around his neck, LIKE A LOON! These facts so obviously point to daffy duck being a loon, that i can't believe they call him daffy DUCK! What do you think?

[Speaking of Loons...]

HI! I'm not wearing any underpants

[Please check - if you smoke too many cigarettes and drink a lot of wine you may be French. There are clinics that can help you recover.]

If I were to pluck my pit hairs and plant them in a Chia Pet, would the hair grow?

[This reader comment was taken out of context, but I think we can safely assume this is one of Alabama's premiere debutantes?]

this is the best stuff i have ever read. i am released from the institution on friday..... can i work for you?

[Actually, half of our staff is on parole]

i can put barbies up my nose!!!!

[Unfortunately, real women won't let you do that.]

I looked at the site asking what I would do if Hurricane Floyd (named after the barber in Andy Griffith Show?) were to come to my state, but my chosen answer was not there. So I will give it here: I would invite Monica Lewinsky to my state and hope that she could suck the life out of Floyd

I am thinking you get paid more that you should, seeing as all you have to do is have a bunch of idiots send in their life stories!

To those who do not like the animal comments, pooh on you. I happen to love animals, their delicious.

[It's like the man said, "If God didn't want us to eat animals, he wouldn't have made them out of meat."]

Hey!!! I can wiggle my nose just like a cute little bunny!

[There are certain lines over which even I will not step.]

TWO TIMES A WEEK!! MOM, TIME TO UP MY RITALIN!

I think the monkeys at the zoo should have to wear sunglasses so they can't hypnotize you.

It's 40 night at the frat house, and the naked midgets are greased and ready to roll.

[When I was in college the worst we ever did was to throw toga parties, get kicked out of school and sabotage the homecoming parade. No wait, I think that was a movie.]

Okay I have a question. After you get a dear john e-mail, how long to you wait to kill the sender?? or maim him, thats okay too.

 [While I can't support manhunting in any form, this is definitely an interesting question. Let me think... pungee sticks? No... Honey and an anthill? No, no... Ah ha! You can subscribe the bastard to Bizarre News. That'll fix his wagon!]

Lewis, I heard that September was National Pleasure Your Spouse Month. Is this true? My husband really wants to know.

[Isn't every month pleasure your spouse month?]

I read that in New York City after a court fight, that a woman can go topless as long as men can and do if they wish. The only time I have seen it in New York on business trips was in the areas of prostitutes hanging out. No, I was not a customer. I was lost on two occasions.

[Sure. A lot of people get lost there.]

I used to work as a DJ at strip clubs, then tried my hand at bartending, retail (In a cosmetics company, the only straight guy there), and each time thought: Wow, I've got the coolest job in the world... That is, until I started getting your column. Basically what I'm trying to say is: You, sir, have the world's coolest job.

[Hey, it's not all Rave parties and penis plants. I've almost been stabbed, robbed, audited (same thing) and abandoned by my wife. Quality journalism is a sacrifice.]

you folks are just sick, nothing in all my life comes close to the perversion you propagate upon the innocents of the world.

[That's our job. Bringing the weird to your mailbox.]

Lewis, you rock more than a autistic kid at a birthday party. Keep up the good work.

[Will the accolades never end?]

I like the Stooges and I'm a girl. Want me to prove it to you?

[Yes. Send me an MPEG of yourself doing the Curly shuffle.]

Great newsletter. You have the only one that I not only read but usually forward to unsuspecting victims....er, I mean family and friends.

Did you notice the headline on a story from Shagmail's People on Monday, Sept. 11th? "COULD BUSH'S CRACK COST HIM AT BALLOT BOX?"

[Looks like someone over there is trying to be funnier than me, and it worked. Thanks, I missed it until now!]

I enjoy your work...but I do not understand what you have against psychics. Why would you not like people like me? Afraid of something you do not understand? Ever made love with an Empath?

[No, but I dated a girl who was a weight-guesser at a carnival, once.]

why not put some bizarre news in about turtles??? i have emailed you at least 4 times now and NO TURTLES!

[When a turtle super-glues its boyfriend s penis to its stomach, I'll be happy to run the story.]

Lewis, The Republic of Nauru is a small island in the pacific, part of Micronesia. It is a bizarre nation as it was predominantly made of bird shit which was mined as super-phosphate most of which was shipped to Australia to be used as fertiliser on crops. -Geoff

[And here I thought I wasn't going to learn anything today.]

7

The Best of Lewis

After reviewing all of the subjects I've tackled during my Bizarre tenure I decided that it would be appropriate to cover some of my favorite moments. It was during this reviewing process that I realized my wife's incredible toleration level! I'm not saying that she handled everything with a twinkle in her eye and a smile on her face, but she realized that my search would entail some questionable pursuits (to say the least). This chapter, more than any, serves as a tribute to the woman behind the man behind the bizarre...and I thank her.

* * *

Greetings fellow Bizarros:

Somehow, many women think me mean-spirited. Every now and then I do pick out the peculiarities in the human race, but rest assured, most of what I write is harmless, even if I am insensitive. Speaking of insensitivities, ever since I got a satellite dish, I often fall asleep with the television on.

With this sleep apnea thing going on, I wake up often. Waking up at 3:00 a.m. with Infomercials hawking their products can be rather disorienting. The other night, I woke up to what I thought was a Saturday Night Live skit, but in reality it was an Infomercial called "Think Big". Featured were twin midgets (or are they called "dwarfs now?) who have made a killing in the real estate market.

I swear it took me five minutes to figure out that this was not some gag take off of the Wizard of Oz. I came into the office and bumped into Chadwick and TZ at the water cooler and mentioned the Infomercial.

Chadwick (the editor of the insults newsletter called Up Yours!) guf-
faws and tells me that he referees midget boxing matches every other
Saturday night at some local bar.

Without going into Chadwick's pathetic social life, he invited me to
experience the rough and tumble world of "Midget Boxing". So I
went. Chadwick was refereeing just like he said...but on his knees. He
told me that he did not want an errant left hook to miss the mark of
an opponent's chin and land squarely in his groin.

Now this was not as bloody as the cockfight in Phoenix, but to see
these little guys with oversized gloves wailing away was at once
pathetic and strangely amusing. In other words: bizarre. Thankfully
nobody got hurt. I was told that this bar went to "Midget Boxing"
after the village outlawed "Midget Tossing".

I can see the e-mail flooding in already about how dare I patronize the
exploitation of little people. To this I say: if you want enlightenment,
subscribe to Quote A Day, otherwise sit back with a cup of java and
enjoy this week's issue of Bizarre News!

Bizarrely yours,

Lewis

Greetings fellow Bizarros:

What an experience! I went to a cockfight the other night. A friend of
a friend had invited me to this illegal affair held in the slums of South
Phoenix. I was the only "gringo" in this warehouse. "Pete" (not his
real name) told me to bring a bottle of tequila to give to the huge
"bouncer" at the door.

The only cockfight I had ever seen before was a scene in Roots, so I
did not quite know what to expect. I had my hands full just hoping I

would get out of the place alive. The thought crossed my mind more than once that journalism in search of the bizarre could get me knifed pretty darn quickly.

I had a great view thanks to Pete. Good enough to get blood all over my clothes. You see they attach these mini blades to the ankles of these roosters (Ok, roosters don't exactly have ankles, but you get the picture.) What ensued was one of the most violent, cruel knife fights I had seen since seeing West Side Story. These huge roosters just went after each other hacking away. All of this amidst a frenzy of betting on which rooster would survive.

Next to me was a gal named Yolanda. She was gorgeous and had on a dress that was more like a second skin. She was amused that I was allowed to experience the event. She was with this huge guy who reminded me of the Frito Bandito. After the third cockfight, a brawl between several of the "guests" broke out until the bouncer tossed them out. I was glad I had TZ's cell phone number in case I needed him to wire money for bail if I got arrested.

In all, I was in this smelly warehouse for two tense hours. The best thing I can say is I survived. After leaving, Pete was hungry and suggested that we get a bite to eat. You guessed it... he wanted chicken.

I drove to LA Monday and plan to stay a few days. I'll fill you in on what adventures await me in this place. Until then, enjoy this edition of Bizarre News.

Bizarrely yours,

Lewis

Greetings Fellow Bizarros:

I heard from my wife and she was not thrilled with my trip to date. It seems experiencing a cockfight and the tattooed lady was not exactly her idea of a business trip. So I decided to skip the truly weird San Francisco. No telling what I would find there. So where the heck am I?

I met a guy in LA who told me he knew of a group of people who had been abducted by aliens. So after a little persuasion here I am, just outside of Area 51. I visited this local place called the A-Le-Inn and asked if they could introduce me to a couple of the people who had been abducted. When I told them I wrote for Bizarre News, this seemed to give me credibility (for the first time in my life I might add!).

I was given two phone numbers of people who believe they had been abducted. Folks, I never believed in this stuff, but that is not important...who cares what I believe in anyway. But "Joe" and "Elaine" (not their real names) actually believe they have been abducted and shared their stories with me. When I started out driving to this place, I thought I would find a weird, (and humorous) story to relay to all of you.

But what I found were two seemingly normal people telling me admittedly weird stories that seemed credible. Now this is bizarre. "Joe" is a 52-year-old male who says he has been abducted more than a dozen times. He says that the "creatures" are using him in some sort of hybrid project to create another species. They do this by draining his sperm and uniting it with an alien embryo.

He doesn't have sex. He said they attach a utensil to his penis that resembles the machine that takes milk from a cow. I couldn't help thinking that Austin Powers might like that machine. He also shared with me the notion that his orgasms last unusually long. To arouse him, they apply some salve to his genitals. When they bring him back, his foreskin sheds like a molting snake's skin.

"Elaine" also has been abducted many times. To hear her tell the story, she is not used for breeding purposes, she is an alien sex slave. "Elaine" is an attractive 30-year-old single lady who doesn't look the type that needs to find an alien to have sex. She says that ever since puberty they have been "taking her up" and having sex with her. She believes that physical relations among aliens are taboo so they need Earthling surrogate sex partners for pleasure.

I couldn't help myself, so I asked her how good was the sex? "Elaine" grew embarrassed but admitted that she has never had an orgasm on earth to rival those with aliens. When I left the interview, I had thought of many other questions. I have their phone numbers and if you want to submit some questions, feel free and I will get back to them when I get back into the office.

Until next issue,

Lewis

Greetings fellow Bizarros:

A computer glitch ate my column for this issue, so I have to wing it because of the deadline. Remarking about television is always an easy target. Last night I saw an HBO special called Real Sex #22. I had never seen this before and presumably there are 21 episodes that ran prior to this one.

This is something like 60 minutes, except instead of anchors; we are treated to all sorts of behind-the-scenes sexual antics. The one story that inspired this segment dealt with sexual dolls. I have been married 12 years, and admittedly lead a rather monk-like life, but this was something beyond the normal. These dolls are not like the ones little girls play with. They cost $5,000 and have silicon breasts (like most women from California), pubic hair woven from actual hair purchased from Holland, and look more real than I thought possible.

The female dolls allowed "entry" into three orifices. No kidding. That's two more than most! The maker said that a lot of people buy these to have a mØnage a trois. I'm sorry but this sort of thing seems a bit weird for me. In the recesses of my decrepit memory, I have faint recollections of a few rather frigid, motionless encounters when I was younger. I guess this is the 21st century's idea of safe sex. As for my own predisposition, give me women that breathe. Strange, they did not have any male dolls for women.

Well, on with this week's issue of Bizarre News. We are edging our way toward the magic 200,000 mark. Thanks for sharing Bizarre News with your friends.

Bizarrely,

Lewis

Greetings fellow Bizarros:

You know we often find a lot of weird stories about "SEX." Howard Stern once remarked that he noticed ratings went up whenever he had "LESBIANS" on his show. We have noticed a remarkable fact that whenever we have stories about "SEX" these issues get forwarded to many more people and we get tons of new subscribers.

Because I want the bosses to send me to Australia for the Olympics and need to get 100,000 more subscribers, I might have to talk about "SEX" more often than I'd like. I am sure all of Australia is mounting a massive unsubscribe campaign to Bizarre News just to keep me away from their island. And how long will it be before the authorities-that-be shut me down in my shameless attempt to build circulation? I don't know, but I found an interesting quote.

"When authorities warn you of the sinfulness of sex, there is an important lesson to be learned. Do not have sex with the authorities." - Matt Groening. Now for those of you who care, Matt is an American cartoonist. But even so, I think his advice is worth taking. The ultimate legal authority in the U.S. is the Attorney General, Janet Reno. Is it me, or is the thought of making love to that woman incomprehensible? If one of her assistants is a reader of this publication I d like to ask him or her, "Would you have sex with Janet Reno to further your career?"

I have heard tell that the First Lady actually likes Ms. Reno more than any of the other people around the President. I think that is because even the President can resist the carnal urges toward her. I really do not intend to be so mean spirited and certainly do not claim to be a gift to women, but Ms. Reno doesn't exactly dress or accentuate her feminine side. Anyway, that's it for my rambling, on with Bizarre News.

Bizarrely,

Lewis

Greetings fellow Bizarros:

Today's subject is simple: Meat. Did you ever wonder what sex the beef you eat was when it was alive? This question touched off a firestorm of controversy in the office. First, Chadwick (Up Yours!) was certain that tender beef had to be from a cow (instead of a bull) because it was tender and had a high fat content...hence was female.

Another in the office suggested that it had to be "bull meat" because cows were too important to slaughter for beef because they were needed for milk and to birth more cattle. One stud bull was enough to satisfy hundreds of females, so the bulls are expendable.

Then Jethro (our latest editorial whiz kid who migrated north to Chicago from Arkansas started his rationale. He suggested that since most people ate their meat toward the "pink side" that it must be female. So Yours Truly decided to find out and called the local Jewel food store and asked to speak to the butcher.

Lewis: Sir, we are calling from Bizarre News and we are having a debate over here on whether the beef meat we eat is mostly cow or bull meat. Can you help me out?

Butcher: Is this a crank call?

Lewis: No sir. While it may be somewhat unconventional to ask, nobody here really knows what sex beef meat normally is.

Butcher: Have you ever turned a rump roast over to check?

Lewis: There are 15 stores within ten miles of here and I have to get the one comic butcher in the area?

Butcher: Actually it depends. Most beef comes from bulls but some comes from cow.

There you have it. The ultimate non-answer. Somehow the idea of eating bull meat is less appealing to me than eating cow. The next time I order a Porterhouse steak, I am sure I ll be thinking about this column.

Bizarrely,

Lewis

Greetings Fellow Bizarros:

I am writing this before Christmas, but you will not be reading this edition until after you have had your fill of eggnog. You know, one of the favorite things in editorial meetings is coming up with the headlines to stories. My favorite of all time was one story about a man who jumped in a snake pit armed with a shotgun. The headline?

------------------ NOT A PIT TO HISS IN -------------------

A reader sent me these headlines. Although I can't actually verify their authenticity, they have the ring of truth. Here are my favorites:

------ Something Went Wrong in Jet Crash, Expert Says -----

------- Police Begin Campaign to Run Down Jaywalkers ------

--------- Is There a Ring of Debris around Uranus? --------

--------------- Prostitutes Appeal to Pope ----------------

------- Panda Mating Fails: Veterinarian Takes Over -------

I would like all of you to pay attention to your local papers and submit your favorite headlines. Please make sure that they are authentic because we cannot verify all of them. We will also have an abbreviated mailing schedule and will be mailing Saturday's edition on Monday, we have not come face to face with Armageddon.

Until Wednesday, enjoy today's dose of the bizarre.

Bizarrely,

Lewis

Greetings Fellow Bizarros:

You know we are all news junkies here. We have to be to come up with the news stories that you are accustomed to reading. Now, how can we pass up the latest "revelations" from Shirley MacLaine? She claims to have had sex with Charlemagne in a past life! She also said that she had sex with a guy named "Olaf" who was a prime minister of one of those Nordic countries.

I am not sure what is more weird; sex with a guy named Olaf or with Charlemagne. Neither exactly roll off the tongue (figuratively speaking). I had a buddy growing up who had a girlfriend named Novella. No kidding. He was quite proud of his first touch of breast (he was in the seventh grade at the time) by wowing her with the line, "Novella my love" and then grabbed her for that first squeeze. For some reason, the free association of writing this column with the thought of Shirley screaming, "Olaf! You stud muffin" took me back to my childhood.

Those precious moments of adolescent passion make for fond memories. Your humble editor even back then seemed to be the chronicler of bizarre moments. Every now and then when a column idea fails me, I will reach back to the past and share one of these moments with you. If you don't like them, scroll down to the stories and skip my rambling.

Lastly, I have been chosen (actually commanded) to become part of the Freebies product team (from GetYourFreebies.com). I have to try all of these free offers and give input as to which free offers actually are good. They had TZ, Clean Laffs Joe, Chadwick (Up Yours!), Simon (Word A Day) and me to get a male perspective. TZ was disqualified because if it is not food or a sex toy, he has nothing to say. Clean Laffs Joe and Simon are rather bland and Chadwick is too mean spirited. So by process of elimination, I have to download all of the free stuff, enter sweepstakes, get samples, etc. and advise. I'll keep you posted on my new responsibilities.

Now, on with the bizarre!

Lewis

Greetings Fellow Bizarros:

Every time I write about an infirmity, we get a ton of e-mail suggesting that I am an insensitive clod. While this might be true, I just have to tell you about the weirdest disease on this planet; Tourettes Syndrome. For those of you who are not familiar with this affliction, this is a disease whereby a person has an uncontrollable tic. The tic most often is a verbal tic whereby the person swears uncontrollably.

So imagine if our President was unfortunate enough to have this affliction. A speech might go something like this:

****

Greetings Fellow (douche bag) Americans:

I speak to you (shit, turd-face, bastards) tonight about a grave (asshole) problem facing our nation (f*$#in' jerk offs). The NRA wants to have me shot...

Now, I have only met one person who definitely had this. When I first met TZ, the editor of Laffaday, I thought he had it. I am not convinced he is free from the disease and all you have to do is spend 15 minutes with him before a string of obscenities fill within earshot. The person who had the disease was Seth Lipschitz. With a name like Lipschitz, having the disease was almost secondary.

You could always count on good old Lipschitz to make an impression. I wonder what he is doing now? What kind of profession could accommodate him? What about an air traffic controller? Priest (or Rabbi in his case)? Someone told me Seth had become a Mambo instructor in Chicago, but this seems highly unlikely. So, I ask you gentle readers, what kind of profession do you think someone with Tourette's would most likely pursue? Send me your suggestions (mailto:Lewis@BizarreNews.com).

Bizarrely,

Lewis

Greetings Fellow Bizarros:

I want to speak to you about sin. Yep, your old editor Lewis wants to moralize a bit. For faithful readers, this might seem odd, but I believe that we actually have a sin worthy of this column: The sin of Onan. We were sitting around the office last night pondering the most bizarre sin, and JA (editor of Quote A Day), came up with this one.

TZ (Laffaday) and I had no clue what this sin of Biblical proportions actually was until JA began to quote the Old Testament. The quote was something like, "Thou shall not spill thy seed upon the Earth." Scripture made masturbation a sin (for at least men.). So, now the word "onanism" has made it into Webster's dictionary. I believe it means "excessive masturbation."

I wonder where in the scale of sin this one actually ranks. I mean, this is not exactly on par with coveting your neighbor's wife, or bearing false witness. Most sin has a bad effect on someone else. But the sin of Onan really harms no one. In fact it might have helped Onan out a few lonely nights. So the deep philosophical quandary is why is this a sin at all? And was spilling your seed on the ground a sin before Onan? What about spilling your seed inside a Playboy magazine? And what about women?

As you see, scripture isn't exactly my strong suit. So the next time you feel like following old Onan's lead, remember to make sure your seed never gets planted in the soil.

Bizarrely,

Lewis

Greetings Fellow Bizarros:

I almost spit out my oatmeal while reading the morning paper the other day. It seems that the annual, Tourrettes Syndrome Golf Outing has been planned for June 19th. The image of 75-100 people golfing while cursing in between and after strokes was an image almost too funny to bear. I thought, what's next? Let me know what kind of bizarre golf outing you would like to attend as a spectator.

But the amusement subsided as I continued to read. This was not an outing for those afflicted but for those raising money for victims of the embarrassing disease.

Your humble editor is not an avid golfer but the last time I did golf, everybody seemed to be cursing before and after every stroke anyway. So the image no longer held its fascination for me as a comical image. But if you are going to be in the area of Riverwoods, IL, drop on by and grab your putter for Tourrettes Syndrome sufferers.

Bizarrely,

Lewis

Greetings Fellow Bizarros:

I have NEVER done anything quite as weird as this. I am typing this at a nudist resort just outside Chicago. A friend of a business colleague is a member and managed to get me a guest pass. I arrived last night and I have to say it was a pleasure not having to unpack much.

It is a warm day and I am nude, sitting with the laptop conveniently covering my private parts. Actually, a laptop gets rather hot and my testicles are sweating more than I ever knew possible.

I walk around this place with a towel. Half the people think that I am a waiter because of the way I have it draped over my arm. I am more shy than I thought. I had thought there would be trouble with embarrassing bouts of arousal, but so far everything is on an even keel. Nerves will do that to you. Everybody seems to pretend that nobody is nude. Yeah, people don't seem to be staring at everybody else's genitalia...except me. I am not turning queer, but I am noticing that a lot of guys have sun screen on their manhood. I did not think to bring anything that would block the sun's rays. I hope I don't get a sunburn down there. That's all I need to do is go home to the wife with my manhood peeling. She will think that I have some exotic venereal disease.

The women here would not exactly get a ticket to Fantasy Island. I had visions of young, nubile nymphs frolicking in the pool like Bo Derek looked in "10." Instead, most of the women look like Hazel in the old B&W television series. Not only are most of them overweight, they are hairy. Hair under their arms (where are we...France?), hair from thigh to thigh, hairy arms...hair everywhere. If I had an electrolysis business, I would set up shop here. I haven't been here that long yet have managed to make an ass out of myself within minutes of walking around. Some guy said "howdy" and I replied, "how's it hanging" and then I broke into a hysterical fit of laughter. He walked away from me as if I was an idiot. Luckily I have access to the Internet from my room. I hope you enjoy this issue filled with the angst of a desperate editor in search of the bizarre. Look for the follow-up next week.

Sweatingly,

Lewis

Greetings Fellow Bizarros:

Thankfully the sun has subsided a bit. Actually it is a bit nippy judging from looking at the women walking around. I never read anything about nudist colony etiquette so I am really like a fish out of water (not that I would actually follow any rules of etiquette anyway.) But the perplexing thing is that there is no place to put your room key. Also, you will never know just how conscious you are of where you place your hands when you are standing in the nude.

This place is filled with sporting activities. I just watch because I am afraid of hurting myself. Running and jumping around butt naked just doesn't look absurd, it feels absurd...trust me on this. There is one lady, about 38-years-old I figure, who has had four children. Her chest looks like two tennis balls stuffed inside a pair of tube socks. She was playing volleyball in the sand. What a sight.

Then there is Wilfred. He is a six-foot nine-inch former basketball player who was playing croquet. I am not sure if he was using a mallet, but he seemed to be drawing a crowd. Now eating in the buff around a circular table with people you do not know is quite an experience. For those of you who do not know me, everybody knows what I eat for lunch by looking at the stains on my shirt.

Now I know why shirts were invented...to keep soup from trickling all the way down to your testicles. It is amazing but it has taken me only two days to become keenly aware of my testicles. No kidding. They get in the way of a lot of stuff. I read somewhere that Sumo wrestlers have a special massage technique. They roll their testicles into their body to save them from being savaged. I should have read up on the technique before dinner!

[Home now and finishing the column...]

Folks, I do not think going around nude is for everybody. I know it is not for me but sharing the experience with you has at least taken the edge off of the ordeal. Now, on with today's issue of Bizarre News.

Clothingly,

Lewis

Greetings Fellow Bizarros:

WARNING: TODAY'S COLUMN IS NOT FOR EVERYBODY. IF SEXUALLY SUGGESTIVE MATERIAL IS OFFENSIVE TO YOU, PLEASE SKIP THE COLUMN AND PROCEED TO THE STORIES.

A lot of columns are inspired by reading the comments you send in. Over the past two weeks, 43 inquiries have been about "face dances." I really had no clue what a "face dance" was but was sure it was something lewd. So I asked TZ and Chadwick, the editors of our lewd publications on jokes and insults. They did not know.

Not being satisfied with the non-answers and my desire to satisfy our readership (and my own growing curiosity), I decided to do research and headed to the all-nude strip joint with TZ. We had been there once before but now, this was being subsidized by the bosses. After a couple of drinks, we both started to loosen up a bit and after being approached by several "dancers", I was ready.

"Excuse me, but can you tell me what a 'face dance' is?" I asked. Irma looked at me and smiled and said, "I can show you a lot better than tell you."

She took my hand and escorted TZ and me to a back room. There was a huge bouncer sitting on a metal chair looking over the room. In each corner women were dancing in the buff for the men. Irma said the cost would be $50 and since it was on the company, I had no problem forking it over.

She asked me to take a dime out of my pocket.

After taking the dime out, she asked me to lie on the floor and place the dime ON MY NOSE. For those of you who don't know me, I have a heck of a honker. I mean I have a real hand full. I am laying on my back with a dime on my nose and Irma straddles my face and proceeds to pick it up off of my nose without her hands, if you get the drift. All the while I hear TZ laughing so hard that he's about to get a hernia.

Then Irma said, "This is a face dance." Now TZ wanted a turn. TZ's nose is rather flat. Actually it is what we call a Roman nose because it "roams" all over his face. When Irma picked up the dime from his nose I thought he was going to choke. That's when I was glad I had a long nose instead of TZ's low profile. There you have it folks. The veil has been lifted from the "face dance."

Bizarrely,

Lewis

Greetings Fellow Bizarros:

Everybody wants to be famous...even if it is only for a fleeting period of time. People do all sorts of crazy things. Have you seen Survivor? Big Brother? (For readers outside the U.S., these are "reality shows" that make real people stars by invading their privacy and making them do goofy stuff.)

But I recently ran across a show in New Zealand while watching an International channel via satellite. I was trying to find programming on Australia and instead chanced upon the neighboring island fare called Havoc 2000 Deluxe. This is a game show of sorts. People do the most bizarre crap I have ever witnessed to win the equivalent of $250 U.S.

I only hope I never have to meet the winners of these kinds of shows. The "winner" of the show I watched was Thomas Hendry. All he did to "win" was staple his penis to a cross 18 times. But he was not done. He then proceeded to pour lighter fluid on his penis and set it on fire.

Don't worry, he doused the fire before any real damage was done to the cross. Once upon a time it was considered bizarre to put out a candle by passing gas. Actually, a guy became famous for this. Now the stakes are higher and a guy has to staple his manhood, set it on fire and then appear on television to become famous. As the edges of taste move further and further we at Bizarre News are there to chronicle this move.

BTW, we crossed the 350,000 mark ahead of schedule. Circulation Director, Jethro has been tracking how many subscribers come to us from passing issues around and says there has been a marked increase in the pass-along rate. Thanks for helping me hit my bonus!

Until Saturday, keep the stapler away from your foreskin.

Bizarrely,

Lewis

Greetings Fellow Bizarros:

Even though we have passed 380,000 subscribers, Bizarre News still gets no respect. I applied for press credentials to get to the Democratic Convention and was denied a press pass. It seems that the powers-that-be over there do not think what I do is "legitimate" reporting.

I admit that what we try to do here is cover the stories that the rest of the country won't touch. For example, there is a rumor that Al Gore has had a hair weave to remove that monk-like bald spot on the back of his head. I wanted to interview Gore's hairdresser to get the low-down. I wanted to do my own expose. There is not much difference between Gore and Bush so the difference will come down to personality...or lack of personality.

I wanted to interview Gore's physician. Why? To confirm if Gore actually has a pulse. I know this sounds weird, but some people actually think that Gore is an alien. Have you ever seen him smile? Looks pretty alien to me. OK...enough of my Gore bashing. Don't think for one moment that I am any more fond of Bush. In fact, I may root for Gore to win the election just so I can write this headline:

Gore Licks Bush.

I am just on a rant because Bizarre News is growing to be one of the largest publications on the Internet and still the old guard will not recognize what we do here. I wanted to bring you the other side of convention coverage. I wanted to take a poll on how many of the delegates actually were not wearing underwear when they cast their vote. Do you think that Dan Rather would tell you that? No way.

Bizarrely,

Lewis

Greetings fellow Bizarros:

Over the weekend TZ and I headed to Vegas. We were celebrating the milestones of Laffaday going over 300,000 subscribers and Bizarre News topping 400,000. We got upgraded on the flight to First Class. After the flight, I think they will rename it "No Class." It all started out with the stewardess asking us if we would like some orange juice.

I politely said that OJ hurt my stomach and asked if they had Tang. TZ, without missing a beat, asked if she could bring him some Tang with "Poon" on the side. While I was laughing hysterically, the lady walked away, disgusted. If there was ever a more goofy looking pair in First Class, I would like to meet them. TZ's reading material consisted of a Benjamin Franklin work called "Fart Proudly."

I gave the wife my word that I would not be doing any reporting from brothels or other "exotic" locations. This was not a working trip, just a time to get away and blow off some steam. But Vegas is Vegas and something unusual always happens. A hooker sat down between TZ and me, trolling for a trick. She ended up leaving with some old guy who was throwing hundred dollar chips around as if they were nickels. It took TZ a while to catch on. He actually thought he was charming her by telling his usual staple of crude jokes.

We managed to play at the tables 17 hours one day, and we each caught one heck of a streak to get us nearly even. We went there with a "system" and every 15 minutes we had to endure insults from fellow gamblers who maintained that we were playing like idiots. I wasn t sure whether they thought that we WERE idiots or simply playing like idiots. Anyway, now that I am home I will be busy cramming for my trip to the Olympics. On with this week's issue of Bizarre News.

Bizarrely,

Lewis

Greetings Fellow Bizarros:

I read a story the other day about a prostitute getting hauled away to jail in Chicago. This certainly is not news, but the twist to the story was that she was in a wheel chair. She was no ordinary "street walker" (bad pun, OK). She would get up to $5,000 for a night of rolling pleasure. I tried to interview her but could not locate a phone number and did not feel like going to 26th and California in Chicago to be at her hearing.

The story got me to thinking about physically challenged prostitutes in other areas. How many blind hookers work the streets? Deaf? I am not making light of infirmities, only when these conditions are coupled with being a hooker. Myself, I would stay away from hookers with colostomy bags.

I just found out recently that prostitution is legal in Sydney. You see, this is the kind of research I do before visiting a place. My wife is thrilled about that. I figure when over there for the Olympics this might make for an interesting column. How many swimmers will take the edge off by visiting a brothel before the big meet? The swimmers from Sweden don't have to worry about this. Everybody knows Swedish swimmers are either gay, sexually permissive or both.

We have a great issue for you today. Thanks for being understanding through our server problems.

Bizarrely,

Lewis

Greetings Fellow Bizarros:

Well, I promised the wife that I would stay away from the Sydney brothel scene, but I broke down after seeing an ad for an "Olympic Special." I did not partake in the carnal pleasures, but simply had to find out how the legal houses of ill repute were making out during this maddening time while visiting Sydney.

I was curious, as any good reporter would be, about their Olympic marketing push. One brothel had three specials:

"Sprints," "Relays" and finally "Marathons." So with notepad in hand (it always helps to at least "look" like a reporter) I visited that brothel. If you were wondering, "Sprints" were for a quick thirty-minute romp with a lady of your choice; "Relays" sounded extremely interesting as a total of four different women would service a patron one after the other. I was told that each "leg" of the relay focused on a different pleasure. Finally, the "Marathon" was for an extended four-hour stint with a single woman.

But the extent of my inquiries was not simply relegated to understanding the clever marketing approach. We have readers from all over the world. Half of you are women, and you will be glad to know that the brothel also had a computer with photos of male studs from which ladies could choose. This was by appointment only, unlike the drop-in traffic off the street for men. I never did see any ladies patronizing the brothel though.

The woman, who ran the place, "Violet", was matronly. She seemed more like a den mother than a lady pedaling sin. I interviewed her about which culture made the place the most money. She told me that hands down, Japanese men made the most money for the house. The reason? It seems (according to "Violet") that most Japanese men finish quicker than other ethnic groups. This means that there is more customer turnover per worker. "Violet" sounded like a CPA. In case you were wondering what ethnic group had the least "turnover", the answer was Australia's own Aborigines. I never found out why.

I asked Violet how they were handling the extra business due to the huge influx of visitors. They had to import prostitutes from all over to accommodate the rush. They sent six prostitutes outside the country to recruit. They were given bonuses for every recruit brought into the country. The thing that struck me about this was how business-like the whole enterprise was. You had the feeling that McDonalds or SONY faced the same challenges as Violet.

For those of you watching the Olympics (from whatever country), I ask you; has this up close and personal story been told to you? Remember, you read it first here! Now, on with the rest of the issue.

Bizarrely,

Lewis

Greetings Fellow Bizarros:

Boy oh boy, did the marital feces hit the fan last week after my wife stumbled on my "research" into the notorious face dance. She doesn't often appreciate my investigative journalism. I went to John, our erstwhile computer geek and asked him to make sure that my wife gets unsubscribed from Bizarre News. I certainly do not want her reading when I go "Down Under" for the Olympics.

Here is a transcript of our brief conversation (from memory since she would have been even more pissed if I got a note pad out and started taking notes.)

WIFE: So, what in the Hell are you doing going to a strip club and having some woman sit on your face for?

Lewis: Honey, it was purely research. Nobody knew what a "face dance" was at the office and before I knew it, I had a dime on my nose.

WIFE: Why do YOU have to do these things? Why can't some single guy find out for you?

LEWIS: They couldn't send Clean Laffs Joe in there; he's a 30-year-old Mormon and still lives with his folks.

WIFE: I can't take this anymore. How am I going to trust you after such an intimate encounter?

LEWIS: You didn't say that after a Doctor shoved his finger up my backside for the exam.

WIFE: Lewis, you're disgusting.

LEWIS: Hey, that is how I got a raise. Would you rather me writing for that local rag again covering the Park District potato sack races?

I think you get the drift. I promised her that bizarre doesn't always equal lewd. For example, I will be visiting an Amish community later in the summer to check out how clean living can become bizarre. The inspiration for the trip came after I heard a joke about what you call an Amish person with his hand stuck up a horse's ass? A mechanic!

We have a great issue for you today that you will want to pass around to some unsuspecting reader.

Bizarrely,

Lewis

Greetings Fellow Bizarros:

Folks, I knew next to nothing about Amish people before making a recent road trip to their community, so I rented the movie "Witness." I thought I would learn all I needed to know from the movie. I expected everyone to be this genteel, caring group, and on the surface that's exactly what I found, barring a certain stiffness they showed toward strangers. But a little patient investigation revealed a rather paranoid group who made a fortune in wooden furniture and illegal drugs.

No fooling. I was approached within my 16 hours at this "village" to purchase cocaine and hashish on two separate occasions. They didn't show this in the movie. There is a younger generation of Amish people who simply do not care for the "old ways" and ride in buggies decked out with portable CD players.

All of this aside, this community is the most inbred looking group I have seen since my trip through Alabama. I think there must only be 20 genes in the entire pool. It's not very surprising if you think about it. A strict lifestyle without electricity, automobiles, or even CNN cannot be recruiting a lot of converts.

I was told about another Amish community that was trying to encourage outsiders to join in order to diversify the gene pool. They must have been running out of second cousins. You have to understand, these people do not have singles bars they can hang out in, and they don't have Internet dating. Even the teenagers with CD stereos in their buggies find it hard to pick up women.

All in all, I do not think that I would want to go back. Hell, after today's column they will never want me back either. I must have asked a hundred questions and didn't buy a single piece of furniture or gram of coke. Anyway, I am glad to be home with my AC, remote control and laptop. Until Saturday, make this week as bizarre as you care to be.

Bizarrely,

Lewis

Greetings Fellow Bizarros:

Something profound is happening in my life. As I have been editing Bizarre News now for over 16 months, weird things happen to me even when I am not seeking them. Such was the case last week when I was audited by the IRS. I filed my own taxes last year because I wanted to save some money. I had some rather "unusual" tax deductions itemized so I was about as nervous as I had ever been in my life.

The IRS audit is an intimidating affair. You feel guilty even when you have nothing to fear. But with my job taking me to a lot of bizarre places, the audit was even more tense because how was I going to explain these legitimate deductions? Before I knew it, I was being interrogated.

IRS Agent: I have to say that I have been auditing returns for eight years and I have never seen these kinds of items deducted from returns. You write for a living?

Lewis: Yes, I am a journalist for an Internet company. (I didn't think he would see the charm of Bizarre News...so I felt a bit awkward.)

IRS Agent: How is it that you believe that you can take a $500 deduction for a 'prostitute in Nevada'?

Lewis: I was researching a story on brothels.

IRS Agent: I see here that you deducted $75 for a 'wager on a cockfight' in Arizona and deducted $112.50 for a round of drinks at the 'Ale-Inn' in New Mexico.

Lewis: I was doing a story about cockfights and needed to wager a bet so I would not stick out. Then I was in Roswell, New Mexico and I needed to interview someone who had been abducted by aliens. I thought that buying a round of drinks would lead to someone introducing me to an abductee. By the way, it worked.

IRS Agent: Do you have any idea just how weird this all is? What kind of job is it exactly that places you into such strange circumstances?

(I was getting the feeling that he did not believe me.)

Lewis: I write a column and edit a publication called Bizarre News.

IRS Agent: (Laughing visibly)... You're THAT Lewis? This IS bizarre because three weeks ago I started reading Bizarre News when I was on vacation in Paris. A friend had forwarded me a copy of your publication. I remember there was a story about a man playing Russian Roulette with an automatic. I subscribed from Paris when I went online over there. I can't believe that you are THAT LEWIS.

Lewis: Well I am glad that you read it. I hope you like it because I have a bunch of new deductions this year.

IRS Agent: Wait until I tell my wife that I audited Lewis at Bizarre News. Are you going to deduct that dime you lost off your nose at the strip club? OK, I will accept all of these deductions.

Wow, the reach of Bizarre News greased the audit for me.

Bizarrely,

Lewis

Greetings Fellow Bizarros:

We have one of the most unusual groups of people here. Each editor is unique and brings that perspective to their craft. Carmen of Great Sexpectations takes a clinical approach to sexual attitudes and mores, TZ (Laffaday) takes the low road, and Clean Laffs Joe doesn't take any road since he might possibly be the only 30-year-old virgin telling jokes on the Net.

Joe actually dates a lot. But yesterday, I heard him talking about his blind date. I thought that he was set up with a stranger he did not know, but he was telling everybody about his date that was literally "blind." This is not the stuff that makes for amusing fair, that was until TZ entered the conversation. It went something like this:

TZ: Joe, how did your date know if you were good-looking?

Joe: She actually ran her hands over my face to get a feel for my features.

TZ: Are you sure she was feeling your face? If she was sitting down and you were standing up, she might have thought your were just a guy with a long nose, baggy eyes and needed a shave...that is if you had your pants pulled down.

Folks, I spit out my coffee all over the two of them. I thought I would share this little story that shows why we have the most unusual group of editors on the Net. Now sit back, relax and savor the world of Bizarre News.

Bizarrely,

Lewis

Greetings Fellow Bizarros:

One of the interesting things about having 378,000 subscribers (and another 100,000 readers who pass this along to friends) is that a lot of people seem to know about Bizarre News. What seems to happen with increasing frequency is the weird things that are introduced to me by friends or "friends of friends." Such was the case last Saturday night.

I was at a company picnic and I met a "friend of a friend" who told me about a party I should go to that would be "perfect" for Bizarre News readers. The party was being held in a deserted warehouse "somewhere on the south side of Chicago." He called it a Rave Party. I had never heard of these parties, but in search of a good column, I met this friend at 10:00 p.m. and headed out to find out what the heck a Rave Party was all about.

Folks, we are into new territory here with this one. As soon as we got there, I believed the cops were sure to follow. To start the ball rolling, a nude lady met us at the door and took us both by the hand into what was to become a modern descent into Dante's Inferno. The music was loud and nasty. The "women" ranged in age from 13 year olds to grandmothers. And the guys - the less said about them the better.

People seemed to be dancing (I think), drinking and groping in every nook and cranny. This was not a place where modesty prevailed. The make-shift bar was a series of plywood sheets propped up on saw-horses. There were so many people by the bar that we were almost shoulder-to-shoulder. I was nervous to speak to anybody except one lady behind the bar. She was outfitted all in leather and looked like she could have been from Eric Von Zipper's gang (from the old Beach Blanket Bingo movies.) But I thought that I would brave an attempt at an interview.

Lewis: So, what do you think of this place?

Lady: Hmmmm. It feels soooo good.

Lewis: Do you come to parties like this often?

Lady: Ahhhhh. Yesssss.

Now I may not be the best interviewer in the world. Heck, I'm no Ted Koppel, but this interview was going nowhere. I remember thinking at the time that she seemed interested in me. But, I kept looking at her eyes, like any good interviewer is supposed to do, and it did not take long to figure out that she wasn't even listening to me.

Lewis: Would you rather that I leave you alone?

Lady: Yes...Yes...YES!

It was then that I realized that standing right behind this lady was some tattooed fellow. At first I thought he was performing some perverted form of dancing, but it soon became obvious that he was having sex with her...during what I thought was an interview. After the shock hit me, I remember feeling distinctly like an idiot for thinking that she was even remotely interested in talking to me. In any case, these parties are not recommended. I was happy to get out of there without getting arrested.

Bizarrely,

Lewis

Greetings Fellow Bizarros:

It's now late at night and I am getting ready to pack for the Sydney Olympics. Some friends and family organized a get together the other day...sort of a "Bon Voyage" party. About 25 people came over to the house, along with the mother-in-law. But despite that, we still had a nice time...until the police crashed our party.

It appears that my mother-in-law read in the newspaper that a white van was seen in the area. The driver is suspected of trying to entice neighborhood kids to take a ride. So when she saw a white van parked in front of the house, she decided to play Agatha Christie and called the police to nab the unsuspecting driver. The only problem was that she failed to ask if the van belonged to anybody at the party. You guessed it...one of our guests had come in that white van. The police were not amused by being led on a wild goose chase.

Anyway, I will finish this column from Sydney...

*****

Well, I made it. The plane ride was one of the most ridiculous trips I ever had. I was trapped in the middle seat for twelve hours, traveling coach (you think that my boss would spring for a First Class ride?). I ended up sitting between a lady with a heavier beard than me and someone with a salivary gland problem. I hadn't seen so much dribbling since I went to see my first Harlem Globetrotters game. And this was in between meals.

The first thing I noticed is that I packed for a "Summer Olympics" and it is cold enough this morning to freeze the balls off a brass monkey. It is early Spring here (because Australia is in the Southern Hemisphere) and I only brought one pair of long pants. Strange, I can tell you where the legal brothels are but I did not bother to check what the average temperature is for mid-September. Priorities are priorities after all. I think I have a line on tickets for the opening ceremonies. I will let you know how they go in Friday s issue. Until then, I remain,

Bizarrely,

Lewis

Greetings fellow Bizarros:

You know, I have to tell you about just how warped this gig is making me. When you spend so much time within the confines of weird, you truly do get off the wall. How you ask? Well, my favorite woman on television happens to be an invisible dream from a Levis jeans commercial. For the readers outside the US, there is a commercial put to the music of Marvin Gay s, "Let's Get It On." An invisible woman does a strip tease leaving nothing but her invisibility to get Yours Truly into a froth. I asked my wife, "Why can't you look like her?" To which she replied, "Lewis, get a hold of yourself, she's invisible! If I looked like her I wouldn't be here, I'd be someplace else."

Yep, an invisible wife - a husband's dream :-)

Bizarrely yours,

Lewis

Greetings fellow Bizarros:

Today's rant is about advertising. I don't know about you, but I get a bit eye weary with all the advertising everywhere! Yeah, I know that we have three ads in every issue to subsidize the publication, but I am talking about advertising ubiquity. For instance, I was eating a banana the other day and the fruit "label" no longer said "Chiquita". The label was an ad for AskJeeves.com!

Every banana had a different banana question. One question was, "How do you know a banana is ripe?" Presumably you need to visit the portal to find out. I myself have a particularly effective way for finding out if a banana is ripe...I take a bite. But that is not the point.

Is nothing sacred anymore? We now have advertising on my bananas. So I wanted to interview the brainchild for this.

The president of the fruit label company is named Irv Weinhaus. I called Irv to find out what it cost to label my banana. Irv wouldn't come clean on the costs. He was an interesting fellow but said that more label advertising was to come, whether I liked it or not. He said that he drew the line when a condom company wanted to advertise on bananas (he was not kidding.) Also he turned away a national bra company that wanted to advertise on melons.

The mind reels with ad possibilities. Anyway, we have a great issue for you this week. Here's to a bizarre week.

Bizarrely yours,

Lewis

Greetings Fellow Bizarros:

Chadwick is the editor of our publication on insults (called Up Yours!). While he tends to be rather a pompous ass most of the time, he does have an idea or two that merit distinction. He suggested that I meet his girlfriend who is into seances. I was surprised when I met her because I was expecting someone who looked more comfortable leaning against a lamp post on Rush Street than the rather normal looking gal she appeared.

She invited me to a seance the other night. If you have never been to one of these, by all means take the opportunity and attend. I was told to be at the JC Motel at 11:00 p.m. sharp.

The neighborhood was not the safest place, but if I could get a column, why not? I soon learned why we were in this seedy hotel room. It seems that "Sue" [who was footing the bill for the evening] wanted to get in touch with her departed husband who, ten years before to the day, had died in the arms of his mistress in the very room we were in.

Chadwick's lady friend was an apprentice channel (he has asked that I not use her name). Herman was the channel conducting the seance. At 11:30, we sat around a table holding hands with a candle and incense burning. After a few minutes, Herman looked as if he was having an epileptic fit. Everybody looked calm and I couldn't help but feel that I was inside a Monty Python skit.

In Saturday's column I will tell you what the results were.....

* * *

Greetings Fellow Bizarros:

Last issue I told you I was at the seance when Herman (the channeler) started to quiver like a New England Shaker. It was just around midnight when Herman began moaning as if he was in the embrace of a woman.

Sue, who was footing the bill, began yelling her dead husband's name. Chadwick sat in the corner smoking one of my cigars and his girlfriend, sitting on my left, began to glance around the room as if she expected the spirit of Houdini himself to appear and start serving drinks.

I was tempted to laugh, but everyone else in the room seemed to be taking it so seriously. Picture a group of adults sitting around a table holding hands, at a dive motel, chanting a dead person's name, with one person sounding like he was having an orgasm at the table. When I seem to be the most normal person in any room...it's a problem.

Herman was really getting into his role, moaning, "Oh, Suzy, I'm waiting for you, Honey!" while he squirmed in his seat.

Sue leaned forward and said, "Jake, is that really you?"

Herman/Jake responded, "It's me Baby. Come here and sit on Daddy's lap." Whereupon Sue broke the circle, stood up and gave Herman an open-handed slap right across the face.

She yelled, "Jake you son-of-a-bitch, I waited ten years to tell you I KNOW you were sleeping with my best friend!"

After she slapped Herman real hard, he stopped the channel. He said the "spirit" left him after the physical contact. I think he was afraid to get another handprint across his face. I left the room with the full belief that Sue had been ripped off for $750. But I guess there's no way to really disprove it. Anyway, we have an issue that will curl your own toes, so sit back, grab a cup of Jo, and enter the world of Bizarre News.

Bizarrely,

Lewis

About ShagMail.com

ShagMail.com is a network of over seventy electronic publications devoted to news, information and entertainment. What makes ShagMail.com so popular is the exclusive original material written by its own stable of talent. Publications like Biography, Clean Laffs, Film & TV Quotes, Great Sexpectations, Forgotten History and Bizarre News are all written by personal editors/writers who imbue each issue with his or her own personality.

ShagMail.com also boasts some of the most popular syndicated material in the country including: Dear Abby, Maggie Gallagher and William F. Buckley.

The best part is that all of this is absolutely free. Feel free to drop by and see why over nine million people a day get their news, information and entertainment from ShagMail.com. We guarantee you'll find something you like.

Visit today:
www.ShagMail.com